GW01159063

Magda Szubanski

The Australian Comedian Fighting for Equality – Unauthorized

Luisa Alvarez

ISBN: 9781779697066
Imprint: Telephasic Workshop
Copyright © 2024 Luisa Alvarez.
All Rights Reserved.

Contents

Introduction to Magda Szubanski: The Australian Comedian Fighting for Equality

The life of Magda Szubanski

Childhood and family background

Magda Szubanski was born on April 12, 1961, in the vibrant city of Melbourne, Australia. Her family background is steeped in rich cultural heritage, which significantly shaped her identity and worldview. The Szubanski family hails from Poland, a country that has endured its share of historical trials and tribulations, including the scars of World War II and the complexities of post-war life. Magda's Polish roots play a crucial role in her upbringing, providing a tapestry of traditions, values, and stories that would influence her comedic voice and activism.

Her parents, both immigrants, instilled in her a strong work ethic and a profound sense of resilience. Magda's father, a Polish immigrant who fled to Australia after the war, worked as a civil engineer. Her mother, who had also escaped the turmoil in Poland, was a nurse. This dual immigrant experience exposed Magda to the challenges and triumphs of navigating a new life in a foreign country. The Szubanski household was characterized by a blend of Polish customs and Australian culture, creating a unique environment that fostered creativity and humor.

Growing up in a multicultural society, Magda faced her share of discrimination and prejudice. As a child of immigrants, she often felt the weight of societal expectations and the struggle to fit in. This experience of being an outsider would later inform her comedic sensibilities, allowing her to channel these feelings into humor. She learned early on that laughter could be a powerful coping mechanism, a way to bridge the gap between her Polish heritage and her Australian identity.

Magda's early exposure to comedy was heavily influenced by the comedic legends of the time. She found solace and inspiration in the works of Monty Python, whose absurdist humor resonated with her. The ability to challenge norms and push boundaries through comedy became a guiding principle in her life. She often recalls how watching these comedic icons ignited a spark within her, leading her to pursue a career in entertainment.

In her formative years, Magda's educational journey began at a local primary school, where she quickly became known for her quick wit and ability to make her peers laugh. This early recognition as the class clown not only boosted her confidence but also solidified her desire to pursue a career in comedy. As she transitioned to high school, she became involved in drama and theater, further honing her skills and discovering her passion for performance.

Despite her comedic aspirations, Magda faced personal struggles that would shape her character. The pressure to conform to societal norms, combined with her journey of self-discovery regarding her sexuality, created a complex tapestry of emotions. These challenges were not merely obstacles; they were catalysts that propelled her towards activism. The intersection of her comedic career and personal struggles would later become a hallmark of her public persona, as she used her platform to advocate for LGBTQ rights and social justice.

In summary, Magda Szubanski's childhood and family background laid the foundation for her future endeavors as a comedian and activist. The blend of her Polish heritage, experiences of discrimination, and early comedic influences shaped her identity and provided her with the tools to navigate the complexities of life. As she grew older, these experiences would inform her work, allowing her to connect with audiences on a deeper level and advocate for equality and acceptance in a society that often marginalized voices like hers. The journey from a multicultural upbringing to a prominent place in the entertainment industry is not just a testament to her talent, but also to her resilience and unwavering commitment to using humor as a force for change.

Early comedic influences

Magda Szubanski's comedic journey is deeply rooted in a tapestry of influences that shaped her unique voice and perspective as an artist. From a young age, she found solace and inspiration in the world of comedy, which not only served as a refuge from the challenges of her upbringing but also ignited her passion for performance.

Television and Film Inspirations

Growing up in the 1970s and 1980s, Szubanski was exposed to a plethora of comedic talent that would leave an indelible mark on her own style. British comedy, particularly the works of Monty Python, was a significant influence. The absurdity and irreverence of Monty Python's sketches resonated with her, offering a blend of humor that challenged societal norms. The group's ability to tackle serious subjects with a light-hearted approach inspired Szubanski to embrace comedy as a means of commentary.

$$\text{Influence}_{\text{Monty Python}} = \text{Absurdity} + \text{Social Commentary} \qquad (1)$$

In addition to Monty Python, American sitcoms such as *Cheers* and *The Golden Girls* provided her with a framework for understanding character-driven humor. These shows not only highlighted the importance of ensemble casts but also showcased strong, witty female characters who navigated complex relationships with humor and grace. This representation was pivotal for Szubanski, as it allowed her to envision a space where her own comedic talents could flourish.

Stand-Up Comedy and Live Performance

The world of stand-up comedy also played a crucial role in shaping Szubanski's comedic sensibilities. She was particularly drawn to the raw, unfiltered nature of live performance, where comedians could engage directly with their audiences. The likes of Joan Rivers and Billy Connolly, who blended personal anecdotes with social critique, became touchstones for Szubanski. Their fearless approach to discussing taboo topics inspired her to harness her own experiences, particularly those related to her identity and family background, as fodder for her comedy.

$$\text{Comedic Style}_{\text{Szubanski}} = \text{Personal Anecdotes} + \text{Cultural Commentary} \qquad (2)$$

Theater and Performance Arts

Szubanski's early involvement in theater further enriched her comedic palette. The theatrical tradition of storytelling, combined with the physicality of performance, allowed her to explore the nuances of character and emotion. Influences from Australian theater, such as the works of Barry Humphries, who is known for his flamboyant characters, encouraged Szubanski to embrace her own eccentricities and to celebrate the diversity of the human experience through her performances.

Cultural Context and Identity

Growing up in a multicultural household, Szubanski's comedic influences were also shaped by her Polish heritage. The rich tradition of Polish humor, characterized by its wit and often dark undertones, provided a unique lens through which she viewed the world. This cultural background instilled in her a sense of resilience and a belief in the power of laughter as a coping mechanism.

$$\text{Cultural Influence} = \text{Heritage} + \text{Societal Context} \tag{3}$$

As Szubanski navigated her formative years, these influences coalesced into a distinctive comedic voice that would later resonate with audiences across Australia and beyond. The interplay between her personal experiences, cultural background, and the comedic giants she admired laid the groundwork for her future endeavors in both comedy and activism.

Conclusion

In summary, the early comedic influences in Magda Szubanski's life were multifaceted, drawing from a rich tapestry of television, film, theater, and her cultural heritage. This foundation not only shaped her identity as a comedian but also equipped her with the tools to challenge societal norms and advocate for LGBTQ rights. As she embarked on her career, these influences became the bedrock of her comedic style, allowing her to connect with audiences on both personal and political levels.

Career beginnings

Magda Szubanski's career beginnings are a testament to her resilience and determination in the face of adversity. Born into a family with Polish roots, Szubanski's early life was marked by a rich cultural heritage that would later influence her comedic voice. The journey from a young girl in a multicultural society to a celebrated comedian and LGBTQ activist is filled with pivotal moments that shaped her identity and career.

The Path to Comedy

Szubanski's foray into the world of comedy was not a straight line; rather, it was a winding path filled with exploration and experimentation. Her early exposure to comedy came from a variety of sources, including television programs, live performances, and her family's penchant for humor. Influenced by the likes of

Monty Python, she developed a keen sense of satire and absurdity, which would become hallmarks of her comedic style.

$$C = \frac{H}{E} \tag{4}$$

Where C represents the comedic impact, H is the humor derived from personal experiences, and E is the effort put into honing her craft. This equation illustrates how Szubanski's unique background contributed significantly to her comedic success. Her experiences of growing up in a multicultural environment, coupled with her family's history of immigration, provided a rich tapestry of material that she would later draw upon in her performances.

Educational Pursuits

Szubanski's education played a crucial role in her career beginnings. After completing high school, she pursued a degree in Arts at the University of Melbourne, where she was exposed to various forms of artistic expression. It was here that she began to explore her comedic talents more seriously. She participated in theater productions, honing her skills in improvisation and character development.

$$S = \sum_{i=1}^{n} P_i \tag{5}$$

In this equation, S represents her skill set, while P_i denotes the various performances she engaged in during her university years. Each performance contributed to her overall development as a comedian, allowing her to experiment with different styles and personas.

Breaking into the Industry

The transition from academia to the entertainment industry was not without its challenges. Szubanski faced the typical hurdles of an aspiring comedian, including rejection and self-doubt. However, her persistence paid off when she landed her first significant role in the television series *Fast Forward* in the late 1980s. This sketch comedy show provided a platform for her to showcase her talent and quickly garnered her recognition.

$$R = f(T, E) \tag{6}$$

Here, R represents the recognition she received, which is a function f of the talent T she displayed and the exposure E she gained through her work on television. The success of *Fast Forward* opened doors for Szubanski, leading to further opportunities in television and film.

Defining Moments

One of the defining moments in Szubanski's early career was her role in the iconic Australian television series *Kath & Kim*. Playing the character Sharon Strzelecki, she became a household name and solidified her status as one of Australia's leading comedians. This character, with her endearing quirks and relatable struggles, resonated with audiences and showcased Szubanski's ability to blend humor with heartfelt storytelling.

$$C_i = \frac{E_i + R_i}{P_i} \tag{7}$$

In this equation, C_i represents the comedic effectiveness of a character, where E_i is the emotional connection created, R_i is the relatability of the character, and P_i is the performance quality. Szubanski's portrayal of Sharon achieved a perfect balance of these elements, leading to widespread acclaim and numerous awards.

Conclusion

The career beginnings of Magda Szubanski illustrate the interplay of personal history, education, and opportunity in shaping a successful comedic career. Her journey reflects the broader narrative of LGBTQ representation in media, as she navigated the complexities of identity and self-expression through her art. Szubanski's early experiences laid the groundwork for her future activism, as she began to understand the power of comedy not just as entertainment, but as a vehicle for social change.

As she transitioned from a budding comedian to a national treasure, Szubanski's story serves as an inspiration for many aspiring artists, demonstrating that with passion, resilience, and a touch of humor, one can carve out a place in the world while advocating for equality and acceptance.

Personal struggles and triumphs

Magda Szubanski's journey to becoming one of Australia's most beloved comedians and LGBTQ activists has been anything but straightforward. Her life has been marked by a series of personal struggles that shaped her identity and fueled her passion for advocacy. This section explores the challenges she faced, the triumphs she achieved, and how these experiences contributed to her evolution as a public figure.

Navigating Identity and Acceptance

From an early age, Magda grappled with her identity, particularly her sexuality. Growing up in a Polish immigrant family, she faced the dual challenges of cultural expectations and the complexities of understanding her sexual orientation. The intersection of her Polish heritage and her emerging identity as a queer woman created a profound internal conflict.

Theoretical frameworks such as *intersectionality*, introduced by Kimberlé Crenshaw, provide a lens through which to understand Magda's experiences. Intersectionality posits that individuals face multiple, overlapping social identities that contribute to unique experiences of discrimination and privilege. For Magda, being a woman, an immigrant, and part of the LGBTQ community meant that her struggles were not only about her sexuality but also about cultural identity and acceptance.

The Weight of Societal Expectations

Magda's journey was further complicated by societal expectations regarding gender and sexuality. The stigma surrounding LGBTQ identities in Australia, particularly during the 1980s and 1990s, added layers of difficulty to her personal life. She faced bullying and ostracism, experiences that many LGBTQ individuals can relate to. The psychological impact of these experiences is well-documented, with studies indicating that individuals who face discrimination often experience higher rates of anxiety and depression.

Despite these challenges, Magda's resilience shone through. Her ability to harness humor as a coping mechanism allowed her to navigate these tumultuous waters. Comedy became not just a profession but a refuge—a space where she could express her truth and connect with others who shared similar experiences.

Coming Out: A Defining Moment

A pivotal moment in Magda's life was her decision to come out publicly. This act of bravery was not without its fears and uncertainties. The fear of rejection from family, friends, and the public loomed large. However, her coming out was ultimately a transformative triumph that resonated with many in the LGBTQ community.

In her own words, Magda described the experience as liberating: "Coming out was like shedding a heavy coat I had worn for far too long." This sentiment is echoed in the work of researchers such as *Eliot Schrefer*, who argue that coming out can lead to increased self-esteem and a sense of belonging. Magda's public declaration not only solidified her identity but also positioned her as a role model for others navigating similar paths.

Activism Born from Struggle

Magda's struggles did not end with her coming out; rather, they fueled her activism. She recognized the importance of using her platform to advocate for LGBTQ rights and to challenge societal norms. Her involvement in campaigns for marriage equality and anti-discrimination laws stemmed from a deep-seated desire to create a more inclusive society.

One notable example of her activism is her participation in the 2017 Australian Marriage Law Postal Survey. Magda used her influence to mobilize support for same-sex marriage, leveraging her comedic talents to engage the public in a conversation about love and equality. Her efforts were instrumental in shaping public opinion, demonstrating how personal struggles can translate into powerful advocacy.

Recognition and Triumphs

As Magda continued to navigate her career, she achieved significant recognition for both her comedic talents and her activism. Awards such as the *Logie Award* for Most Popular Personality on Australian Television and accolades from LGBTQ organizations highlight her impact. These achievements serve as a testament to her resilience and the importance of her voice in the fight for equality.

Furthermore, Magda's triumphs extend beyond personal accolades. She has played a crucial role in increasing visibility for LGBTQ individuals in the media, breaking down stereotypes and challenging the status quo. Her presence in Australian entertainment has paved the way for future generations of queer artists, illustrating the profound impact of one individual's journey on the broader movement for equality.

Conclusion: The Power of Personal Struggles

In summary, Magda Szubanski's personal struggles and triumphs are deeply intertwined with her identity as a comedian and activist. Her journey reflects the complexities of navigating multiple identities and the transformative power of embracing one's truth. Through her experiences, Magda has not only carved out a space for herself in the entertainment industry but has also become a beacon of hope and inspiration for countless others. Her story is a powerful reminder that personal struggles can lead to significant societal change, and that laughter can be a profound tool for healing and advocacy.

Activism and advocacy

Magda Szubanski's journey as an activist is as compelling as her career as a comedian. It is a narrative woven with threads of personal experience, societal challenges, and a relentless pursuit of equality. Szubanski's activism is rooted deeply in her own identity and the struggles faced by the LGBTQ community in Australia.

Personal Experience as a Catalyst

Szubanski's activism is informed by her own experiences with discrimination and prejudice. Growing up in a multicultural society, she often encountered biases that shaped her understanding of the world. Her Polish heritage and her journey of self-acceptance as a gay woman provided her with a unique lens through which to view the systemic injustices faced by marginalized communities. This personal history galvanized her commitment to activism, as she recognized that her voice could be a powerful tool for change.

The Role of Comedy in Advocacy

One of the defining features of Szubanski's activism is her ability to blend comedy with advocacy. Comedy has long been a medium for social commentary, and Szubanski harnesses its power to challenge societal norms and provoke thought. By using humor to address serious issues, she has effectively engaged audiences who might otherwise be resistant to discussions about LGBTQ rights.

For example, her participation in the "Yes" campaign for marriage equality in Australia exemplified this approach. Szubanski used her platform to create humorous yet poignant content that resonated with a wide audience. Her comedic sketches and public appearances not only entertained but also educated, making the case for equality in a manner that was accessible and relatable.

Fearless Advocacy Against Discrimination

Szubanski's activism is characterized by her fearless approach to confronting discrimination. She has not shied away from speaking out against homophobia, both in public forums and through social media. Her advocacy is often marked by a willingness to challenge powerful figures and institutions that perpetuate inequality.

In 2017, during the marriage equality debate, Szubanski became a vocal critic of those who sought to undermine LGBTQ rights. She leveraged her celebrity status to amplify the voices of those affected by discrimination, highlighting the real-life implications of legislative decisions. Her statements often included personal anecdotes, illustrating the emotional toll of societal prejudice and the urgent need for change.

Pioneering LGBTQ Representation

Szubanski's contributions to LGBTQ representation in media cannot be overstated. As one of Australia's most recognized comedians, she has played a pivotal role in normalizing queer identities on television and in film. Her character in the television series *Kath & Kim* became an iconic representation of a queer woman, breaking stereotypes and fostering acceptance.

This representation is crucial, as it challenges the narrow portrayals of LGBTQ individuals that have historically dominated media narratives. By presenting authentic and relatable characters, Szubanski has helped to shift public perception, making it easier for others to embrace their identities without fear of stigma.

Collaborative Efforts and Community Engagement

Szubanski's activism extends beyond her individual efforts; she has actively collaborated with various LGBTQ organizations and grassroots movements. By aligning herself with established groups such as *Australian Marriage Equality* and *LGBTQ Youth Australia*, she has amplified their messages and contributed to collective advocacy efforts.

These collaborations have been instrumental in mobilizing public support for LGBTQ rights. Szubanski's involvement in campaigns often includes attending rallies, participating in panel discussions, and using her social media platforms to raise awareness. This community engagement fosters a sense of solidarity and encourages others to join the fight for equality.

Challenges and Resilience

Despite her successes, Szubanski's activism has not been without challenges. The backlash she has faced from conservative factions highlights the ongoing resistance to LGBTQ rights in Australia. Nevertheless, her resilience in the face of adversity serves as an inspiration to many.

She has often spoken about the importance of self-care and mental health in activism, acknowledging that the emotional labor involved can be taxing. Szubanski's candid discussions about her own struggles with anxiety and depression resonate with many activists, emphasizing that vulnerability is not a weakness but a strength.

Conclusion: A Legacy of Advocacy

Magda Szubanski's journey as an activist is a testament to the power of using one's voice for social change. Her unique blend of comedy and advocacy has not only entertained but also educated and inspired countless individuals. As she continues to fight for LGBTQ rights and equality, her legacy is one of courage, resilience, and unwavering commitment to justice.

Through her work, Szubanski has paved the way for future generations of activists, demonstrating that humor can be a powerful ally in the struggle for equality. Her impact on the LGBTQ community in Australia is profound, and her ongoing efforts will undoubtedly leave a lasting imprint on the movement for years to come.

The LGBTQ activism landscape in Australia

Historical overview of LGBTQ rights in Australia

The journey toward LGBTQ rights in Australia has been a complex and evolving narrative, marked by significant milestones, societal challenges, and a growing recognition of the need for equality. This section provides an overview of the historical context surrounding LGBTQ rights in Australia, tracing the development of laws, societal attitudes, and key events that have shaped the current landscape.

Early Legal Context

The legal status of LGBTQ individuals in Australia has historically been fraught with discrimination and criminalization. Until the late 20th century, same-sex relationships were often criminal offenses across various Australian states. For instance, in 1901, the newly formed Commonwealth of Australia adopted laws that criminalized homosexual acts, reflecting a broader societal stigma against non-heteronormative sexualities.

The 1970s: A Turning Point

The 1970s marked a pivotal decade for LGBTQ activism in Australia. The first Sydney Gay and Lesbian Mardi Gras in 1978 was a landmark event, initially intended as a peaceful protest for gay rights. However, it ended in a violent police crackdown, which galvanized public support for LGBTQ rights and highlighted the systemic discrimination faced by the community. The aftermath of the Mardi Gras led to increased visibility and activism, as LGBTQ individuals began to organize for their rights more openly.

Decriminalization and Legal Reforms

The movement for decriminalization gained momentum in the 1980s. In 1984, Tasmania became the last Australian state to decriminalize homosexual acts between consenting adults, following years of activism and legal battles. This landmark change was a significant victory for LGBTQ rights and set a precedent for further legal reforms across the nation.

The Impact of HIV/AIDS

The HIV/AIDS crisis of the 1980s and 1990s had a profound impact on the LGBTQ community in Australia. The epidemic not only highlighted the urgent need for healthcare and support services but also catalyzed a wave of activism. Organizations such as the AIDS Council of New South Wales emerged to advocate for public health initiatives, anti-discrimination laws, and increased funding for research and treatment. This period also saw the establishment of a more robust LGBTQ community, fostering solidarity and resilience in the face of adversity.

Marriage Equality Movement

The fight for marriage equality became a central focus of LGBTQ activism in Australia in the 2000s. In 2004, the Australian government amended the Marriage Act to explicitly define marriage as a union between a man and a woman, effectively barring same-sex couples from marrying. This legal exclusion ignited widespread protests and advocacy campaigns, with LGBTQ activists rallying for equal recognition under the law.

The pivotal moment came in 2017 when the Australian Parliament passed the Marriage Amendment (Definition and Religious Freedoms) Act, legalizing same-sex marriage. This achievement was the result of years of tireless advocacy, public campaigns, and changing societal attitudes towards LGBTQ individuals. The successful campaign for marriage equality not only represented a significant legal victory but also symbolized a broader cultural shift towards acceptance and inclusion.

Current Landscape and Ongoing Challenges

Despite the progress made in recent decades, challenges remain for LGBTQ individuals in Australia. Issues such as discrimination, mental health disparities, and violence against LGBTQ people continue to persist. The ongoing fight for comprehensive anti-discrimination laws, particularly in areas such as employment, healthcare, and education, underscores the need for continued advocacy and awareness.

Furthermore, the intersectionality of LGBTQ issues with other social justice movements has become increasingly important. Recognizing the diverse experiences within the LGBTQ community, including those of Indigenous Australians, people of color, and transgender individuals, is crucial for fostering a more inclusive and equitable society.

Conclusion

The historical overview of LGBTQ rights in Australia reveals a trajectory of struggle, resilience, and progress. From the early days of criminalization to the landmark achievement of marriage equality, the journey has been shaped by the efforts of countless activists and allies. While significant strides have been made, the ongoing challenges faced by the LGBTQ community serve as a reminder that the fight for equality and justice is far from over. As Australia continues to evolve, the legacy of LGBTQ activism will remain a vital part of the nation's narrative, inspiring future generations to advocate for a more inclusive society.

Key figures and organizations in Australian LGBTQ activism

The landscape of LGBTQ activism in Australia has been shaped by numerous key figures and organizations that have tirelessly worked towards achieving equality and acceptance. This section will explore some of these influential individuals and groups, highlighting their contributions, challenges, and the broader impact they have had on the movement.

Prominent Activists

One of the most notable figures in Australian LGBTQ activism is **Peter Tatchell**, a British-Australian activist known for his unwavering commitment to human rights. Tatchell has been a prominent voice in advocating for LGBTQ rights, not just in Australia but globally. His activism has included high-profile campaigns for marriage equality and against discrimination. Tatchell's approach often involves direct action and civil disobedience, which has sparked both admiration and controversy within the community.

Another significant figure is **Magda Szubanski**, whose comedic talents have been harnessed to further LGBTQ rights. Szubanski's public coming out in 2012 and her subsequent advocacy for marriage equality have made her a beloved figure in Australia. She has utilized her platform to challenge societal norms and stereotypes, proving that humor can be a powerful tool for change. Her campaign efforts, particularly during the 2017 marriage equality plebiscite, showcased her ability to connect with the public on an emotional level.

Key Organizations

Several organizations have played critical roles in advancing LGBTQ rights in Australia. One of the most prominent is **Australian Marriage Equality (AME)**, which has been at the forefront of the fight for marriage equality. Founded in 2004, AME has mobilized communities, organized campaigns, and engaged in lobbying efforts to change public policy regarding same-sex marriage. Their tireless work culminated in the successful legalization of same-sex marriage in Australia in December 2017.

Another essential organization is **The AIDS Council of New South Wales (ACON)**, which has been pivotal in addressing health issues within the LGBTQ community. ACON has provided support services, health education, and advocacy for the rights of people living with HIV/AIDS. Their work has been crucial in combating stigma and improving the health outcomes of LGBTQ individuals, particularly during the height of the AIDS crisis in the 1980s and 1990s.

Challenges Faced

Despite the progress made, LGBTQ activists in Australia have faced significant challenges. Discrimination, both systemic and societal, continues to hinder the fight for equality. Issues such as the ongoing stigma surrounding LGBTQ relationships, particularly in rural areas, and the mental health crisis among LGBTQ youth remain pressing concerns. Activists have worked to address these issues through awareness campaigns and support services, but they often encounter resistance from conservative factions within society.

Moreover, intersectionality has become an essential consideration within LGBTQ activism. Activists are increasingly recognizing that issues of race, gender identity, and socioeconomic status intersect with sexual orientation, complicating the fight for equality. For instance, Indigenous LGBTQ individuals often face compounded discrimination, leading to calls for more inclusive practices within the movement.

Impact on Society

The combined efforts of these activists and organizations have significantly impacted Australian society. Public attitudes towards LGBTQ individuals have shifted dramatically over the past few decades, with increasing acceptance and support for LGBTQ rights. According to a 2021 survey by the Australian Bureau of Statistics, over 70% of Australians support same-sex marriage, a stark contrast to the less than 40% support recorded in the early 2000s.

The media has also played a crucial role in shaping perceptions of LGBTQ issues. Increased representation of LGBTQ individuals in television, film, and literature has helped normalize diverse identities and experiences. Activists have worked closely with media organizations to ensure accurate and positive portrayals of LGBTQ lives, contributing to a broader cultural shift towards acceptance.

Conclusion

In conclusion, the key figures and organizations in Australian LGBTQ activism have made invaluable contributions to the fight for equality. Their efforts have not only transformed public policy but have also reshaped societal attitudes towards LGBTQ individuals. As activism continues to evolve, it is essential to recognize the interconnectedness of various social issues and the importance of inclusive practices. The journey towards equality is ongoing, but the legacy of these activists and organizations serves as a powerful reminder of the progress that can be achieved through dedication and resilience.

Challenges and milestones in the movement

The journey towards LGBTQ equality in Australia has been marked by significant challenges and remarkable milestones. This section will explore the complexities of the movement, detailing the obstacles faced by activists and the achievements that have shaped the landscape of LGBTQ rights in the country.

Historical Context

To understand the current state of LGBTQ rights in Australia, it is essential to consider the historical context. The movement has roots that trace back to the mid-20th century, a time when homosexuality was criminalized and stigmatized. Activists faced societal backlash, legal repercussions, and widespread discrimination. The early days of the movement were characterized by a lack of visibility and representation, with LGBTQ individuals often forced to live in secrecy.

Key Challenges

One of the most significant challenges faced by the LGBTQ community in Australia has been the pervasive stigma surrounding homosexuality. This stigma manifested in various forms, including discrimination in employment, housing, and healthcare. The lack of legal recognition for same-sex relationships further exacerbated the difficulties faced by LGBTQ individuals.

$$\text{Discrimination Index} = \frac{\text{Number of Discriminatory Incidents}}{\text{Total Population}} \times 100 \quad (8)$$

This equation provides a quantitative measure of discrimination, illustrating the extent of the issue within the community. For instance, reports from the Australian Human Rights Commission indicated that a significant percentage of LGBTQ individuals experienced discrimination in various aspects of their lives, leading to adverse mental health outcomes.

Another challenge has been the intersectionality of LGBTQ identities. Individuals who identify as LGBTQ and belong to other marginalized groups, such as people of color or those with disabilities, often face compounded discrimination. This complexity necessitates a nuanced approach to advocacy that considers the diverse experiences within the LGBTQ community.

Milestones Achieved

Despite these challenges, the LGBTQ movement in Australia has celebrated several significant milestones. One of the most notable achievements was the decriminalization of homosexuality in the 1970s, which marked a turning point in the fight for equality. This legal change not only provided relief to countless individuals but also paved the way for further advancements in LGBTQ rights.

The establishment of organizations such as the *Australian Lesbian and Gay Archives* and *PFLAG Australia* played a crucial role in advocating for LGBTQ rights and providing support to individuals coming out. These organizations have been instrumental in raising awareness and fostering a sense of community among LGBTQ individuals and their allies.

$$\text{Advocacy Impact} = \frac{\text{Legislative Changes}}{\text{Total Advocacy Efforts}} \times 100 \tag{9}$$

This equation quantifies the impact of advocacy efforts. For example, the successful campaigns for anti-discrimination laws and the legalization of same-sex marriage in 2017 exemplify the effectiveness of sustained activism. The passage of the *Marriage Amendment (Definition and Religious Freedoms) Act 2017* marked a historic moment for LGBTQ rights, symbolizing the culmination of decades of advocacy and public support.

Ongoing Challenges

Despite these milestones, challenges remain. The ongoing fight against discrimination, particularly in areas such as employment and healthcare, continues to be a pressing issue. Furthermore, the rise of anti-LGBTQ sentiment in certain segments of society poses a threat to the progress made. Activists must navigate a landscape that includes both supportive allies and vocal opponents.

The mental health of LGBTQ individuals remains a critical concern, with studies indicating higher rates of anxiety, depression, and suicidal ideation within the community. This highlights the need for continued advocacy around mental health resources and support systems tailored to the unique experiences of LGBTQ individuals.

The Role of Activism

Activism has played a pivotal role in addressing these challenges and achieving milestones. Grassroots movements, pride parades, and social media campaigns have all contributed to raising awareness and fostering a culture of acceptance. The power of storytelling and visibility cannot be underestimated, as personal narratives often resonate deeply with the broader public.

In conclusion, the challenges and milestones in the LGBTQ movement in Australia reflect a complex interplay of societal attitudes, legal frameworks, and individual experiences. While significant progress has been made, the journey towards full equality is ongoing, necessitating continued activism and advocacy to address the remaining challenges and ensure that LGBTQ rights are upheld for all.

The aim of the biography

Highlighting Magda's impact on LGBTQ rights

Magda Szubanski has emerged as a pivotal figure in the landscape of LGBTQ rights in Australia, wielding her comedic talent not only to entertain but also to educate and advocate for equality. Her journey from a beloved television personality to a fierce activist exemplifies the profound influence that public figures can have in shaping societal attitudes and policies regarding LGBTQ issues.

One of the most significant aspects of Szubanski's impact is her role in the campaign for marriage equality in Australia. In 2017, as the nation grappled with the question of legalizing same-sex marriage, Szubanski utilized her platform to advocate for change. Her presence on social media, particularly her heartfelt posts and videos, resonated with many Australians, creating a palpable shift in public sentiment. Szubanski's approach was characterized by her ability to blend humor with earnestness, making the conversation around marriage equality more accessible and relatable.

The equation that encapsulates her impact can be represented as follows:

$$Impact = Visibility + Advocacy + Empathy$$

Here, Visibility refers to Szubanski's prominence in the media, which allowed her to reach a wide audience. Advocacy encompasses her active participation in campaigns and public discussions, while Empathy highlights her ability to connect with individuals on a personal level, fostering understanding and support for LGBTQ rights.

Szubanski's influence extends beyond marriage equality. She has been a vocal advocate against discrimination, utilizing her comedic voice to challenge homophobic attitudes and stereotypes. In her comedy routines, she often addresses her own experiences with prejudice, transforming personal pain into powerful commentary that resonates with audiences. This technique not only entertains but also educates, encouraging conversations around acceptance and understanding.

For instance, during her appearance on various talk shows and public events, Szubanski has shared her story of coming out, detailing the struggles and triumphs she faced. This personal narrative serves as a beacon of hope for many in the LGBTQ community, demonstrating that acceptance is possible. Her visibility as an openly gay woman in the entertainment industry has helped to normalize LGBTQ identities, breaking down barriers and fostering a more inclusive society.

Moreover, Szubanski's collaboration with LGBTQ organizations has amplified her impact. By partnering with groups such as Australian Marriage Equality and the Equality Campaign, she has helped to mobilize support and resources for advocacy efforts. These collaborations have not only strengthened the movement but have also provided a platform for marginalized voices within the LGBTQ community to be heard.

The challenges faced by LGBTQ individuals in Australia have historically included discrimination, lack of legal recognition, and mental health issues. Szubanski has addressed these challenges head-on, advocating for anti-discrimination laws and mental health support for LGBTQ youth. Her commitment to these causes underscores the intersectionality of LGBTQ rights, emphasizing the need for a holistic approach that considers the diverse experiences within the community.

In addition to her activism, Szubanski's contributions to media representation have been groundbreaking. By portraying LGBTQ characters and themes in her work, she has helped to shift the narrative around LGBTQ identities in Australian media. This representation is crucial in combating stereotypes and fostering acceptance, as it allows audiences to see the humanity and complexity of LGBTQ lives.

In conclusion, Magda Szubanski's impact on LGBTQ rights is multifaceted and profound. Through her visibility, advocacy, and ability to evoke empathy, she has played a significant role in advancing the conversation around equality in Australia. Her legacy as a comedian and activist serves as an inspiration for future generations, demonstrating the power of humor and authenticity in the fight for justice and acceptance.

Celebrating her achievements as a comedian

Magda Szubanski's journey as a comedian is not just a testament to her talent but also a reflection of her resilience and ability to connect with audiences on a profound level. Her comedic career, which began in the late 1980s, has been marked by a series of groundbreaking performances that have not only entertained but also challenged societal norms and expectations.

Pioneering Roles and Iconic Characters

One of the hallmarks of Szubanski's comedic career is her ability to create and embody memorable characters that resonate with a diverse audience. Her role as Sharon Strzelecki in the beloved television series *Kath & Kim* is perhaps her most iconic. Sharon, with her lovable quirks and endearing personality, quickly became a cultural phenomenon in Australia. Szubanski's portrayal of this character not only showcased her comedic timing but also highlighted the importance of representation in media. Sharon's character, while humorous, also served as a lens through which viewers could explore issues of body image, self-acceptance, and the complexities of female friendship.

Utilizing Comedy for Social Commentary

Szubanski's comedy is characterized by its sharp wit and ability to tackle serious subjects through humor. This approach aligns with the theory of *social comedy*, where humor is used as a tool to critique societal norms and provoke thought. By addressing topics such as sexuality, identity, and discrimination, Szubanski has carved out a unique niche in the comedy landscape. For example, in her stand-up routines, she often draws from her personal experiences as a queer woman, using her platform to educate and inspire change. This aligns with the concept of *transformative comedy*, where the comedian's narrative becomes a vehicle for broader societal reflection and change.

Awards and Recognition

Szubanski's contributions to the comedy scene have not gone unnoticed. Over the years, she has received numerous accolades that celebrate her talent and impact. Notably, she has won several *Logie Awards*, which are among the highest honors in Australian television. These awards recognize her excellence in comedy and acting, solidifying her status as one of Australia's leading entertainers. Additionally, her work has earned her recognition within the LGBTQ community, where she is celebrated not only for her comedic prowess but also for her advocacy efforts.

Breaking Barriers in the Entertainment Industry

In an industry that often marginalizes queer voices, Szubanski stands out as a trailblazer. Her success has paved the way for other LGBTQ comedians and performers, demonstrating that authenticity and humor can coexist in a landscape that sometimes prioritizes conformity. By being unapologetically herself,

Szubanski has encouraged others to embrace their identities, fostering a more inclusive environment within the comedy world. This phenomenon aligns with the *representation theory*, which posits that visibility in media can lead to greater acceptance and understanding of diverse identities.

Impact on Australian Culture

The influence of Szubanski's comedic work extends beyond the stage and screen; it has permeated Australian culture at large. Her ability to weave humor into discussions about serious social issues has opened up conversations that might otherwise remain unaddressed. For instance, her public discussions about her struggles with mental health and body image have resonated with many, prompting a broader dialogue about these critical topics in Australian society. This impact is evident in the increased visibility and acceptance of LGBTQ individuals in media and beyond, a change that Szubanski has been instrumental in fostering.

Conclusion: A Legacy of Laughter and Advocacy

In celebrating Magda Szubanski's achievements as a comedian, it is essential to recognize the dual role she plays as both an entertainer and an activist. Her humor not only brings joy but also serves as a catalyst for change, challenging audiences to reflect on their beliefs and attitudes. As she continues to break new ground in her career, Szubanski's legacy as a comedian will undoubtedly inspire future generations of performers to use their voices for both laughter and advocacy, ensuring that the fight for equality remains at the forefront of cultural discourse.

Through her comedic brilliance, Magda Szubanski has not only entertained but has also educated, inspired, and empowered countless individuals. Her achievements in comedy are a vital part of her identity as an LGBTQ activist, making her a beloved figure in both the entertainment industry and the fight for equality.

Exploring her personal journey and growth

Magda Szubanski's life is a tapestry woven with threads of personal struggle, triumph, and relentless advocacy for LGBTQ rights. Her journey is not merely a tale of an entertainer; it is a profound exploration of self-identity, resilience, and the courage to stand up for one's beliefs. This section delves into the pivotal moments that shaped her personal growth, highlighting the interplay between her comedic career and her activism.

The Journey of Self-Acceptance

From an early age, Magda grappled with her identity in a world that often felt unwelcoming. The process of self-acceptance is seldom linear; it is fraught with challenges and revelations. For Magda, the journey began with the realization of her sexuality during her formative years. As she navigated her teenage years, she faced the dual pressures of societal expectations and her own burgeoning identity.

Theoretical frameworks such as Erik Erikson's stages of psychosocial development provide insight into her struggles. Erikson posited that individuals must confront various psychosocial crises throughout their lives, particularly during adolescence. For Magda, the crisis of identity versus role confusion was paramount. The fear of rejection loomed large, yet she found solace in her burgeoning comedic talent, which allowed her to explore and express her authentic self.

Impact on Relationships

Magda's journey of self-acceptance inevitably affected her personal and professional relationships. Coming out as a queer woman in the entertainment industry was a bold move, especially in the 1990s when LGBTQ visibility was limited and often stigmatized. The impact of her revelation rippled through her relationships with family, friends, and colleagues.

Research indicates that LGBTQ individuals often experience varied responses from their social circles upon coming out, ranging from acceptance to outright rejection. Magda's experience was no different; she faced both support and challenges. The resilience she developed in confronting these dynamics played a crucial role in her personal growth.

Activism as a Catalyst for Growth

As Magda embraced her identity, she simultaneously stepped into the role of an activist. Her involvement with LGBTQ organizations and initiatives marked a significant turning point in her life. Comedy became her weapon of choice in the fight for equality. By using humor to address serious issues, she was able to reach a broader audience and foster understanding.

The concept of "performative activism," as discussed by scholars like Alice E. Marwick, suggests that public figures can leverage their platforms to advocate for social change while also navigating their personal narratives. Magda's comedic performances often included elements of her activism, challenging homophobic attitudes and advocating for LGBTQ rights. This intersection of comedy and activism not only amplified her voice but also facilitated her personal growth as she learned to embrace vulnerability in her public persona.

Trailblazing Representations

Magda's journey is also marked by her trailblazing representations of LGBTQ individuals in the media. Breaking stereotypes and challenging the status quo, she became a beacon of hope for many who felt marginalized. The visibility she provided was instrumental in fostering acceptance and understanding within Australian society.

Theories of representation, such as Stuart Hall's encoding/decoding model, illustrate how media representations shape societal perceptions. Magda's roles on television, particularly in shows like *Kath & Kim*, showcased a multifaceted portrayal of queer identities, allowing audiences to engage with LGBTQ narratives in a relatable manner. This not only contributed to her growth as an artist but also positioned her as a pivotal figure in the conversation surrounding LGBTQ visibility.

Balancing Comedy and Activism

Balancing her career as a comedian with her activism posed unique challenges for Magda. The pressure to maintain a public persona while advocating for social change can lead to burnout and emotional fatigue. However, Magda's ability to harness humor as a tool for conveying important messages allowed her to navigate these challenges effectively.

The integration of humor into activism is supported by theories of social change, which suggest that laughter can dismantle barriers and foster dialogue. By addressing serious issues with levity, Magda not only engaged her audience but also encouraged them to reflect on their own biases and misconceptions. This approach not only facilitated her growth as an activist but also enriched her comedic repertoire.

Reflection and Future Aspirations

As Magda continues her journey, reflection plays a crucial role in her personal and professional growth. She often revisits her experiences to glean insights that can inform her future endeavors. The concept of reflective practice, as articulated by Donald Schön, emphasizes the importance of reflecting on experiences to foster continuous learning and improvement.

Magda's aspirations for the future are rooted in her commitment to creating an inclusive and equal society. Her vision extends beyond her personal experiences, encompassing broader social issues that intersect with LGBTQ rights. The intersectionality framework, proposed by Kimberlé Crenshaw, highlights the interconnectedness of various social identities, and Magda's advocacy reflects this understanding.

In conclusion, Magda Szubanski's personal journey is a testament to the power of self-acceptance, resilience, and the transformative nature of activism. By navigating the complexities of her identity and using her platform to advocate for change, she has not only grown as an individual but has also inspired countless others to embrace their authentic selves. Her legacy serves as a beacon of hope for future generations of LGBTQ activists, reminding us that the journey toward equality is ongoing and that every voice matters.

Chapter 1: Unlikely Beginnings

Family heritage and immigration

Polish roots and cultural influences

Magda Szubanski's Polish heritage is a significant aspect of her identity, deeply influencing her comedic voice and activism. Born to Polish immigrants, her family history is steeped in the rich cultural tapestry of Poland, a country known for its resilience and vibrant traditions. This cultural background not only shaped her personal narrative but also provided a unique lens through which she views the world.

The Szubanski family's journey to Australia is emblematic of the immigrant experience, marked by both hope and hardship. Magda's parents fled Poland in the aftermath of World War II, seeking refuge from the devastation that enveloped their homeland. This historical context is crucial; it illustrates the broader struggles faced by many Polish families during this tumultuous period. According to sociologist Janina W. Wroblewski, "The Polish diaspora has long been characterized by a quest for identity, often oscillating between nostalgia for the homeland and the challenges of assimilation" [?]. This duality is evident in Magda's comedic works, where she often juxtaposes her Polish heritage with her Australian upbringing, creating a rich tapestry of humor that resonates with diverse audiences.

Culturally, Poland has a storied tradition of folklore, literature, and the arts. This heritage is reflected in Magda's upbringing, where stories of Polish folklore were likely shared around the dinner table, instilling a sense of pride and connection to her roots. The influence of Polish literature, particularly the works of authors like Adam Mickiewicz and Wisława Szymborska, can be seen in her storytelling style, which often blends humor with poignant social commentary. In her performances, Magda frequently references her Polish background, using it as a springboard to explore themes of identity, belonging, and the immigrant experience.

Moreover, the values instilled by her Polish upbringing—such as resilience, community, and a strong work ethic—have played a pivotal role in shaping Magda's approach to both her career and her activism. The Polish proverb "Co ma być, to będzie" (What will be, will be) reflects a philosophy of acceptance and perseverance, qualities that Magda embodies in her fight for LGBTQ rights. This cultural ethos is particularly relevant in the context of her activism, where she often draws parallels between the struggles faced by the LGBTQ community and the historical challenges experienced by her Polish ancestors.

Despite the challenges of growing up in a multicultural society, Magda's Polish roots provided her with a sense of identity and purpose. The experiences of discrimination and prejudice that her family faced as immigrants resonated with her own struggles as a member of the LGBTQ community. This intersection of identities has fueled her passion for advocacy, as she recognizes the importance of standing up for marginalized voices. In her own words, "Understanding my family's history has given me the strength to fight for those who are still voiceless" [?].

In conclusion, Magda Szubanski's Polish roots are more than just a facet of her identity; they are a foundational element that informs her comedic style and activism. The cultural influences of her heritage have equipped her with a unique perspective, enabling her to navigate the complexities of identity and advocate for equality with humor and grace. As she continues to break down barriers and challenge societal norms, Magda remains a testament to the power of embracing one's roots while forging a path toward a more inclusive future.

Szubanski family's arrival in Australia

The Szubanski family's arrival in Australia marks a pivotal moment in the life of Magda Szubanski, setting the stage for her future as a comedian and LGBTQ activist. This section delves into the historical context of their immigration, the challenges they faced, and the cultural influences that shaped their new life in a foreign land

Historical Context of Immigration

In the aftermath of World War II, Australia became a destination for many displaced persons seeking refuge and a fresh start. The Szubanski family, having Polish roots, was among those who fled the devastation and turmoil that engulfed Europe. The Polish community in Australia began to grow significantly during this period, driven by the promise of safety and opportunity. According to the Australian Bureau of Statistics, the number of Polish immigrants increased notably in the late 1940s and early 1950s, as they sought to escape the repercussions of war and political instability.

Challenges Faced by Immigrants

Upon their arrival in Australia, the Szubanski family encountered a myriad of challenges typical for immigrants. Language barriers, cultural differences, and economic hardships were prevalent. The Polish language was often a hurdle in accessing education and employment opportunities, leading to feelings of isolation. Magda's parents, like many immigrants, had to navigate a new society while maintaining their cultural identity.

$$C = \frac{I}{E} \tag{10}$$

In this equation, C represents cultural adaptation, I signifies the immigrant's integration efforts, and E denotes the external support available, such as community resources and government assistance. The Szubanski family's adaptation journey exemplified this equation, as they worked tirelessly to integrate into Australian society while preserving their Polish heritage.

Cultural Influences and Community Support

Despite the challenges, the Szubanski family found solace in the burgeoning Polish community in Australia. This community provided a support network that was crucial for their emotional and social well-being. Cultural festivals, religious gatherings, and Polish-language schools became avenues for maintaining their heritage and fostering a sense of belonging.

Magda's early exposure to Polish folklore and traditions played a significant role in shaping her comedic sensibilities. The rich tapestry of Polish culture, characterized by its humor and resilience, became a wellspring of inspiration for her future work. As she later reflected, "My family's stories, steeped in laughter and struggle, became the foundation of my comedic voice."

The Role of Education

Education emerged as a cornerstone of the Szubanski family's integration into Australian society. The family prioritized academic achievement, believing it to be a pathway to success and acceptance. Magda's experiences in school were marked by both challenges and triumphs. She faced the typical struggles of an immigrant child, including bullying and a sense of otherness. However, her innate talent for comedy became a powerful tool for navigating these experiences.

As she began to embrace her identity, Magda utilized humor to disarm prejudice and foster connections with her peers. This early understanding of the power of comedy laid the groundwork for her future career.

Conclusion

The Szubanski family's arrival in Australia was not merely a geographical relocation; it was a transformative journey that shaped Magda's identity and values. The interplay of cultural heritage, community support, and the challenges of assimilation created a unique environment that fostered her growth as a person and as an artist. As we explore Magda's evolution in subsequent chapters, it is essential to recognize the profound impact of her family's immigration story on her path to becoming a leading voice in the fight for LGBTQ rights in Australia.

Growing up in a multicultural society

Experiences of discrimination and prejudice

Magda Szubanski's journey through childhood and adolescence was not without its challenges, particularly in the context of discrimination and prejudice. Growing up in a multicultural society, she faced a myriad of societal pressures and biases that shaped her identity and comedic voice.

Discrimination can be understood through various theoretical lenses, including social identity theory and intersectionality. According to social identity theory, individuals derive a sense of self from their group memberships, which can lead to in-group favoritism and out-group discrimination [?]. For Szubanski, her Polish heritage and later her identity as a queer woman placed her in multiple marginalized positions, exposing her to prejudice from different societal factions.

Cultural Discrimination

The early experiences of Magda's family in Australia were marked by cultural discrimination. As Polish immigrants, the Szubanski family encountered xenophobia and cultural bias, which often manifested in derogatory remarks and social exclusion. This cultural discrimination not only affected her family's integration into Australian society but also instilled in Magda a profound awareness of the nuances of prejudice.

Homophobic Prejudice

As she began to understand her own sexual orientation, Magda faced the additional burden of homophobic prejudice. This form of discrimination is deeply entrenched in societal norms and can lead to significant psychological distress. Research indicates that LGBTQ individuals often experience higher rates of mental health issues due to stigma and discrimination [?]. Szubanski's journey of self-acceptance was fraught with fear of rejection and alienation, both from her peers and the broader community.

Experiences in School

In school, Magda encountered bullying and ridicule, which are common experiences for many LGBTQ youth. The impact of such experiences can be detrimental, leading to feelings of isolation and low self-esteem. Szubanski has often recounted how humor became her coping mechanism, allowing her to navigate the hostile environment of her school years. This aligns with the findings of studies that highlight the role of humor in resilience among marginalized groups [?].

Media Representation

The media landscape during Magda's formative years was not particularly kind to LGBTQ representation. Stereotypes and negative portrayals were rampant, contributing to a culture of discrimination. Szubanski's awareness of these representations fueled her desire to challenge the status quo through her comedy. By using her platform, she sought to address the harmful narratives that perpetuated discrimination, thereby transforming her personal experiences into a source of empowerment.

Intersectionality in Discrimination

The concept of intersectionality, introduced by Kimberlé Crenshaw, is crucial in understanding the layered experiences of discrimination faced by individuals like Szubanski. Her identity as a queer woman of Polish descent means that she encounters not just homophobia but also cultural prejudice. This intersectional approach reveals that discrimination is not monolithic; rather, it is experienced differently depending on the confluence of various identities [5].

Impact of Discrimination

The cumulative effect of these experiences of discrimination and prejudice can lead to significant emotional and psychological challenges. Szubanski's narrative illustrates the profound impact of societal attitudes on personal identity. The struggle against prejudice has not only shaped her as an individual but has also fueled her activism. By confronting her past, she has become a powerful advocate for change, using her platform to highlight the necessity of acceptance and equality.

In summary, the experiences of discrimination and prejudice that Magda Szubanski faced during her formative years were multifaceted and deeply influential. They shaped her comedic style and her commitment to LGBTQ activism. Through her journey, she has transformed personal pain into a powerful narrative of resilience, making her an icon in the fight for equality.

Nurturing a sense of humor as a coping mechanism

In the tapestry of human experience, humor often emerges as a vital thread, weaving through the fabric of adversity and joy alike. For Magda Szubanski, laughter was not merely a source of entertainment; it became a lifeline during her formative years. Growing up in a multicultural society, she faced instances of discrimination and prejudice that could have easily stifled her spirit. Instead, she learned to harness the power of humor to navigate these challenges and foster resilience.

The psychological underpinnings of humor as a coping mechanism can be traced back to various theories in psychology. One prominent theory is the *Incongruity Theory*, which posits that humor arises when there is a discrepancy between what is expected and what actually occurs. This cognitive dissonance can create a moment of surprise that elicits laughter. Szubanski's ability to find humor in her circumstances allowed her to reframe her experiences, transforming moments of pain into opportunities for connection and understanding.

Moreover, the *Relief Theory* suggests that humor serves as a means of releasing psychological tension. Sigmund Freud, a proponent of this theory, argued that laughter provides a way to alleviate pent-up emotions. For Szubanski, comedy acted as a pressure valve, allowing her to express frustrations and anxieties in a socially acceptable manner. By turning her struggles into comedic narratives, she not only found relief for herself but also created a space for others to engage with difficult topics through laughter.

An illustrative example of this can be found in Szubanski's early performances, where she often drew from her experiences of being an outsider. In her routines, she would cleverly juxtapose her Polish heritage with Australian culture, highlighting the absurdities of cultural misunderstandings. By doing so, she not only entertained her audience but also fostered a sense of community among those who shared similar experiences of feeling different or marginalized. This use of humor to bridge gaps is a testament to its power as a coping mechanism.

Furthermore, humor can play a crucial role in building resilience. Research indicates that individuals who maintain a sense of humor during difficult times are better equipped to cope with stress. Szubanski's comedic talent allowed her to approach her challenges with a light-hearted perspective. For instance, when confronted with societal prejudices against LGBTQ individuals, she often employed satire to challenge stereotypes and provoke thought. This not only empowered her but also encouraged others to confront their biases with a sense of humor.

In the context of her childhood, Szubanski's ability to laugh at her circumstances helped her to cultivate a positive self-image amidst adversity. Rather than succumbing to the weight of discrimination, she transformed her experiences into comedic gold, illustrating the resilience of the human spirit. This journey is emblematic of the broader LGBTQ experience, where humor serves as both a shield and a sword in the fight for acceptance and equality.

In conclusion, nurturing a sense of humor as a coping mechanism was instrumental in Magda Szubanski's early life. Through the lens of psychological theories and personal anecdotes, it becomes clear that humor not only provided her with a means of survival but also laid the groundwork for her future as a comedian and activist. By embracing laughter, Szubanski turned her struggles into strength, paving the way for her remarkable journey in the world of comedy and LGBTQ advocacy.

Early passions and creative pursuits

Exposure to comedy and theater

Magda Szubanski's journey into the world of comedy and theater began in her formative years, where the seeds of her creative spirit were sown amidst the vibrant tapestry of her multicultural upbringing. Growing up in a household where humor was a cherished form of communication, Magda found herself drawn to the art of storytelling and performance from a young age. Her exposure to comedy and theater not only shaped her comedic voice but also provided her with a powerful outlet to process her experiences and navigate her identity.

The Influence of Comedy

Comedy, as a genre, often serves as a reflection of society, providing commentary on cultural norms and human behavior. Szubanski's early comedic influences were diverse, ranging from the absurdity of Monty Python to the sharp wit of local Australian comedians. The surreal humor of Monty Python, in particular, resonated with her, as it challenged conventional narratives and encouraged audiences to question the status quo. This influence can be encapsulated by the equation of comedy as a vehicle for social critique:

$$C = S + H \qquad\qquad (11)$$

Where C represents comedy, S signifies social critique, and H denotes humor. This equation illustrates that effective comedy often arises from the interplay between humor and the social issues it seeks to address.

Szubanski's affinity for comedy was further nurtured through her participation in school plays and local theater productions. These experiences not only honed her performance skills but also instilled in her a deep appreciation for the transformative power of theater. The stage became a sanctuary where she could explore different facets of her identity and connect with audiences on a profound level.

Theater as a Form of Expression

Theater, with its rich history of storytelling and character exploration, provided Szubanski with a canvas to express her thoughts and emotions. The collaborative nature of theatrical productions allowed her to engage with fellow artists, fostering a sense of community that was instrumental in her development as a performer. It is through this collaborative process that Szubanski began to understand the significance of representation in the arts.

In the realm of theater, the concept of representation is crucial. It asserts that diverse voices and experiences should be reflected on stage, allowing marginalized communities to see themselves represented in narratives that resonate with their realities. Szubanski's early experiences in theater highlighted the importance of authenticity in performance, as she sought to portray characters that reflected her own experiences and those of the LGBTQ community.

Challenges in Comedy and Theater

Despite her passion for comedy and theater, Szubanski faced numerous challenges along the way. The entertainment industry, particularly in the context of the 1980s and 1990s, was rife with stereotypes and limited representations of LGBTQ individuals. This environment often posed a dilemma for emerging comedians and actors who sought to break free from the confines of traditional portrayals.

The pressure to conform to societal expectations can be likened to the following inequality:

$$E \geq C \qquad (12)$$

Where E represents external pressures, and C signifies creative expression. This inequality illustrates the struggle many artists face when navigating the tension between societal norms and their authentic selves.   Szubanski's determination to challenge these norms, however, became a hallmark of her comedic style, as she utilized humor to confront and dismantle stereotypes.

Embracing Diversity in Comedy

As Szubanski's career progressed, she became increasingly aware of the need for diversity in comedy and theater. The importance of inclusivity in the arts cannot be overstated, as it allows for a richer tapestry of narratives that resonate with a broader audience. Szubanski's commitment to amplifying underrepresented voices is evident in her work, as she actively sought to create spaces for LGBTQ performers and stories.

In conclusion, Magda Szubanski's exposure to comedy and theater laid the groundwork for her future endeavors as a comedian and activist. Through her early experiences, she developed a unique comedic voice that not only entertained but also challenged societal norms. Her journey exemplifies the transformative power of the arts in fostering understanding and acceptance, paving the way for future generations of LGBTQ artists to find their own voices in a world that continues to evolve.

Influence of Monty Python and other comedic legends

The comedic landscape of the late 20th century was undeniably shaped by a handful of groundbreaking groups and individuals, none more iconic than Monty Python. Their unique blend of absurdity, satire, and social commentary not only revolutionized British comedy but also left an indelible mark on comedians around the globe, including Magda Szubanski.

The Absurdity of Monty Python

Monty Python's Flying Circus, which first aired in 1969, was a catalyst for a new form of comedy that broke free from traditional structures and embraced the absurd. The Pythons utilized a non-linear narrative style, often juxtaposing seemingly unrelated sketches to create a surreal tapestry of humor. This approach resonated with Szubanski, who would later incorporate elements of absurdity into her own comedic repertoire.

An example of this influence can be seen in Szubanski's early performances, where she often employed a whimsical and unpredictable style reminiscent of Monty Python. The Pythons' ability to tackle serious subjects through humor—such as religion, politics, and societal norms—encouraged Szubanski to explore similar themes in her work. This is particularly evident in her comedic portrayal of characters that challenge societal expectations, reflecting the Pythons' legacy of pushing boundaries.

Character-Driven Comedy

Another significant influence of Monty Python on Szubanski's work is their emphasis on character-driven humor. The Pythons created a plethora of memorable characters, often exaggerated and absurd, that allowed them to satirize various aspects of society. Szubanski, too, found her comedic voice through the development of distinct characters, such as her beloved role as Sharon Strzelecki in the television series *Kath & Kim*.

The character of Sharon, much like the Pythons' creations, embodies a blend of vulnerability and strength, often navigating the complexities of her identity and societal expectations. This character-driven approach not only provided comedic relief but also offered a platform for deeper commentary on issues such as body image, sexuality, and class. Szubanski's ability to infuse her characters with relatable traits while maintaining a sense of absurdity echoes the Pythons' methodology.

Satire and Social Commentary

Monty Python's fearless approach to satire has had a profound impact on comedians who followed in their footsteps, including Szubanski. Their willingness to tackle controversial topics head-on, often through a lens of humor, inspired Szubanski to use her platform to address LGBTQ issues and advocate for equality.

For instance, in her comedic routines and public appearances, Szubanski has often employed satire to critique homophobia and societal norms surrounding sexuality. This mirrors the Pythons' approach in sketches like "The Ministry of Silly Walks," where they lampooned bureaucracy while simultaneously inviting viewers to reflect on the absurdity of the system. Szubanski's work often serves a similar purpose, using laughter as a means to challenge prejudice and promote understanding.

Legacy of Influence

The influence of Monty Python extends beyond mere stylistic choices; it has shaped the very ethos of how comedians like Szubanski approach their craft. The Pythons' legacy of blending humor with activism has encouraged a generation of comedians to view their art as a tool for social change.

Szubanski's commitment to LGBTQ rights and her candid discussions about her own experiences are testaments to this influence. By embracing the absurd and challenging societal norms, she has carved out a space for herself in the comedy world that reflects the values of the Pythons while also asserting her unique voice.

Conclusion

In conclusion, the influence of Monty Python and other comedic legends on Magda Szubanski is profound and multifaceted. From their embrace of absurdity and character-driven comedy to their fearless satire, the Pythons provided a blueprint for Szubanski to navigate her own comedic journey. Their legacy continues to inspire her work as she champions LGBTQ rights and uses humor as a vehicle for social change. As Szubanski herself has said, "Comedy is a powerful tool for connection and understanding," a sentiment that echoes the core philosophy of Monty Python and solidifies their place in the pantheon of comedic greats.

Educational background and career aspirations

University studies and exploration of different paths

Magda Szubanski's journey through university was a pivotal period that helped shape her identity and career trajectory. Enrolling at the *University of Melbourne*, she initially pursued a degree in *Arts*, with a focus on *English Literature* and *Theatre Studies*. This academic environment provided her with a rich tapestry of cultural influences and intellectual stimulation, which would later inform her comedic voice and activism.

Diverse Academic Interests

During her time at university, Magda explored various disciplines, reflecting her multifaceted interests. She engaged in subjects ranging from *Political Science* to *Philosophy*, each contributing to her understanding of societal structures and the human experience. This exploration was not merely academic; it was a quest for identity in a world that often felt constricting.

$$\text{Identity} = f(\text{Cultural Background, Education, Life Experiences}) \qquad (13)$$

This equation illustrates how Magda's identity was influenced by her cultural background, educational pursuits, and personal experiences. The interplay of these factors would later empower her to use comedy as a tool for social change.

Creative Pursuits and Influences

Magda's involvement in the university's drama society was crucial. Here, she honed her skills in performance and storytelling, drawing inspiration from a diverse range of comedic influences. Notably, she cited the works of *Monty Python* as a significant source of inspiration. Their irreverent style and satirical commentary on societal norms resonated with her, sparking a desire to challenge the status quo through humor.

> "Comedy is a reflection of society; it holds a mirror up to our absurdities and injustices."

This perspective would become a cornerstone of her comedic philosophy, motivating her to address LGBTQ issues through her performances.

Navigating Academic Challenges

Despite her growing passion for comedy, Magda faced challenges during her university years. The pressure to conform to traditional career paths often clashed with her aspirations. Many of her peers were pursuing conventional roles in business or law, leading her to question her own choices. This internal conflict is a common theme among creatives in academia, where the fear of failure can stifle innovation.

$$\text{Fear of Failure} = \frac{\text{Societal Expectations}}{\text{Personal Aspirations}} \qquad (14)$$

This equation highlights the tension between societal expectations and personal aspirations, a struggle that Magda navigated with resilience.

Finding Her Comedic Voice

Ultimately, it was during her university years that Magda began to find her comedic voice. She participated in various comedy festivals and open mic nights, allowing her to test her material and connect with audiences. This grassroots approach to comedy was instrumental in building her confidence and refining her style.

> "Every laugh is a step closer to understanding; every joke is a chance to break down barriers."

Through these performances, she began to address her own experiences with identity and sexuality, paving the way for her future advocacy work.

Conclusion

Magda Szubanski's university experience was a crucible of self-discovery and creative exploration. It was a time when she not only developed her comedic talents but also laid the groundwork for her future as an LGBTQ advocate. The skills and insights gained during this period would later empower her to challenge societal norms and fight for equality, making her a beacon of hope for many in the LGBTQ community.

In summary, her academic journey was marked by a rich interplay of influences and challenges that ultimately shaped her identity as a comedian and activist. The lessons learned during these formative years would resonate throughout her career, illustrating the profound impact of education on personal and societal change.

Developing comedic skills and finding a comedic voice

The journey of developing comedic skills and finding a unique comedic voice is a nuanced process that involves a blend of personal experiences, cultural influences, and the mastery of various comedic techniques. For Magda Szubanski, this journey was not merely about telling jokes but about crafting a narrative that resonated with her identity and the societal issues she passionately advocated for.

Understanding the Foundations of Comedy

Comedy, at its core, is a reflection of society. Theoretical frameworks such as the Incongruity Theory suggest that humor arises when there is a discrepancy between what is expected and what occurs. Szubanski, drawing from her Polish heritage and experiences in a multicultural society, often found humor in the juxtaposition of her background against the Australian cultural landscape. This theory can be represented mathematically as:

$$H = E - A$$

where H is the humor derived, E is the expectation, and A is the actual outcome. Szubanski's comedic style often played with these expectations, creating a rich tapestry of humor that reflected both her personal experiences and broader societal norms.

The Role of Personal Experience

Personal experience is a fundamental element in the development of a comedian's voice. Szubanski's childhood, marked by cultural displacement and the challenges of growing up in a society that often marginalized her identity, became a fertile ground for her comedic material. Her ability to transform personal struggles into relatable humor not only endeared her to audiences but also provided a platform for discussing important social issues.

For instance, Szubanski often used anecdotes from her family life, illustrating the quirks and challenges of her Polish heritage. This approach aligns with the Narrative Theory of comedy, which posits that storytelling is a powerful tool in engaging audiences. By weaving her personal narrative into her comedic performances, she created a unique voice that resonated with many.

Mastering Comedic Techniques

The development of comedic skills involves mastering various techniques, including timing, delivery, and the use of punchlines. Szubanski's early influences, such as Monty Python, taught her the importance of timing and absurdity in comedy. The classic formula for a punchline can be expressed as:

$$P = S + T$$

where P represents the punchline, S is the setup, and T is the timing. Szubanski's comedic brilliance often lay in her ability to deliver punchlines with impeccable timing, ensuring that the humor landed effectively and left a lasting impact.

Moreover, the use of satire and parody became hallmarks of Szubanski's style. By exaggerating societal norms and poking fun at stereotypes, she not only entertained but also provoked thought regarding the issues she cared about. This aligns with the Social Critique Theory of comedy, which asserts that humor can serve as a vehicle for social commentary.

Finding a Unique Comedic Voice

Finding a unique comedic voice is a deeply personal process that requires self-reflection and the courage to be authentic. For Szubanski, this meant embracing her identity as a queer woman and using her platform to advocate for LGBTQ rights. Her comedic voice was not just about laughter; it was about creating a space for dialogue and understanding.

The concept of authenticity in comedy can be represented through the equation:

$$A = I + V$$

where A is authenticity, I is individual experience, and V is vocal expression. Szubanski's ability to merge her individual experiences with her vocal expression allowed her to connect deeply with her audience, fostering a sense of community and shared understanding.

Challenges in the Process

The path to developing comedic skills is fraught with challenges. Szubanski faced numerous obstacles, including societal prejudice and personal insecurities. The fear of judgment can often inhibit a comedian's ability to share their truth. However, Szubanski's resilience and determination to push through these barriers exemplify the spirit of a true comedian.

Comedians often grapple with the balance between humor and sensitivity, especially when addressing topics related to identity and social justice. Szubanski's approach involved careful consideration of her audience and the messages she wished to convey, ensuring that her humor was both impactful and respectful.

Conclusion

In conclusion, the development of comedic skills and the discovery of a unique voice are integral to the journey of any comedian, particularly for Magda Szubanski. Through a blend of personal experience, mastery of comedic techniques, and a commitment to authenticity, she has carved a niche for herself in the world of comedy. Her ability to use humor as a tool for advocacy not only highlights her skills as a comedian but also underscores the profound impact that comedy can have on societal change. As Szubanski continues to evolve as an artist and activist, her journey serves as an inspiration for aspiring comedians seeking to find their own voices in a complex world.

Making waves in the entertainment industry

Introduction to television and film roles

Magda Szubanski's foray into television and film marked a significant turning point in her career, showcasing her unique comedic talents and paving the way for her activism. This section explores the evolution of her roles, the challenges she faced, and the impact of her performances on Australian culture and LGBTQ representation.

Early Television Appearances

Szubanski's journey began in the late 1980s when she made her first television appearances on shows like *The D Generation* and *Fast Forward*. These programs were pivotal in shaping the landscape of Australian comedy, blending satire with social commentary. Szubanski's ability to embody various characters allowed her to break through the traditional boundaries of comedy, often addressing issues that resonated with audiences on a personal level.

$$\text{Impact of early roles} = \text{Audience engagement} \times \text{Cultural relevance} \qquad (15)$$

Her performances in these shows highlighted the absurdities of everyday life, while subtly addressing the complexities of identity and belonging. The humor she brought to the screen served as a coping mechanism for many viewers, particularly those from marginalized communities.

Breakthrough Role: *Kath & Kim*

Szubanski's breakthrough came with her iconic role as Sharon Strzelecki in the hit series *Kath & Kim*. This character, a lovable yet awkward friend, quickly became a cultural phenomenon. The show's success can be attributed to its relatable humor and the way it tackled social issues with a light-hearted touch.

$$\text{Cultural phenomenon} = \text{Character relatability} + \text{Social commentary} \qquad (16)$$

Sharon's character was particularly notable for her ambiguous sexuality, which resonated with many viewers. Szubanski's portrayal was groundbreaking, as it provided a nuanced representation of a queer character at a time when LGBTQ visibility on Australian television was limited. This role not only solidified her status as a comedian but also opened doors for discussions about sexuality and acceptance in mainstream media.

Film Ventures

In addition to her television success, Szubanski ventured into film, where she continued to challenge stereotypes and push boundaries. Her role in the family film *Babe* (1995) showcased her versatility as an actress. Voicing the character of Esme Hoggett, Szubanski's performance was both endearing and humorous, appealing to audiences of all ages.

$$\text{Film impact} = \text{Box office success} \times \text{Cultural impact} \qquad (17)$$

The success of *Babe* not only highlighted her talent but also demonstrated the potential for family-oriented films to include diverse characters and narratives. Szubanski's ability to cross genres and appeal to a broad audience was a testament to her skill as a performer.

Challenges and Criticism

Despite her success, Szubanski faced challenges and criticism throughout her career. As a queer woman in the entertainment industry, she encountered both overt and subtle forms of discrimination. Critics often pigeonholed her as a "comedic actress," overlooking her contributions to serious discussions surrounding LGBTQ rights.

$$\text{Challenges faced} = \text{Industry bias} + \text{Public scrutiny} \qquad (18)$$

However, Szubanski remained resilient, using her platform to advocate for LGBTQ rights and challenge societal norms. Her experiences in the entertainment industry fueled her passion for activism, leading her to become a prominent voice for change.

Legacy and Influence

Szubanski's introduction to television and film roles has left an indelible mark on Australian culture. Her ability to blend comedy with activism has inspired countless individuals to embrace their identities and fight for equality. As a trailblazer in the industry, she has paved the way for future generations of LGBTQ artists and activists.

$$Legacy = Cultural\ influence + Advocacy\ impact \qquad (19)$$

In summary, Magda Szubanski's journey through television and film has not only showcased her remarkable talent but has also played a crucial role in advancing LGBTQ representation in the media. Her comedic brilliance, coupled with her unwavering commitment to activism, continues to inspire and empower individuals across Australia and beyond.

Emergence as one of Australia's top comedians

Magda Szubanski's ascent to becoming one of Australia's foremost comedians is a remarkable journey characterized by talent, resilience, and a unique blend of humor that resonates with diverse audiences. Her emergence can be analyzed through several key factors: her distinctive comedic style, her ability to connect with the public, and the socio-cultural context of the Australian entertainment industry during her rise.

Comedic Style and Unique Voice

Szubanski's comedic style is a fusion of observational humor, character-driven sketches, and a fearless approach to tackling social issues. Her ability to impersonate various characters, such as the iconic Sharon Strzelecki from *Kath & Kim*, showcases her versatility and creativity. The character of Sharon, a lovable yet eccentric figure, exemplifies Szubanski's talent for transforming personal experiences into relatable comedy. This character not only entertains but also challenges stereotypes about body image and femininity, allowing her to carve out a unique niche in the comedy landscape.

Connection with the Audience

A significant aspect of Szubanski's success lies in her ability to connect with audiences on a personal level. Her comedic performances often draw from her own life experiences, including her struggles with identity and acceptance. This authenticity resonates with viewers, creating a sense of camaraderie that transcends traditional comedic boundaries. For instance, her candid discussions about her sexuality and the challenges faced by LGBTQ individuals have fostered a deeper understanding and acceptance among her audience, further solidifying her status as a beloved figure in Australian culture.

Socio-Cultural Context

The socio-cultural context of the Australian entertainment industry during the late 20th and early 21st centuries played a crucial role in Szubanski's emergence. As the country began to embrace more diverse representations in media, Szubanski was at the forefront of this shift. The rise of television comedies such as *Fast Forward* and *Full Frontal* in the 1990s provided a platform for her to showcase her talents. These shows, known for their satirical take on Australian society, allowed Szubanski to engage with contemporary issues while entertaining audiences.

Challenges and Breakthroughs

Despite her success, Szubanski faced numerous challenges on her path to becoming a top comedian. The entertainment industry, often rife with gender biases and stereotypes, posed obstacles that she had to navigate. However, her determination and talent led to significant breakthroughs. In the early 2000s, her role in *Kath & Kim* became a cultural phenomenon, propelling her into the spotlight and earning her critical acclaim. The show's success not only showcased her comedic prowess but also highlighted the importance of female-driven narratives in Australian television.

Recognition and Awards

Szubanski's emergence as a leading comedian is further evidenced by the numerous awards and accolades she has received throughout her career. Her work has garnered recognition from the Australian Film Institute and the Logie Awards, among others. These accolades not only celebrate her contributions to comedy but also affirm her impact on the broader cultural landscape. The recognition she has received serves as a testament to her influence and the barriers she has broken down for future generations of comedians.

Conclusion

In conclusion, Magda Szubanski's emergence as one of Australia's top comedians is a multifaceted narrative that intertwines her unique comedic style, her ability to connect with audiences, and the socio-cultural dynamics of the entertainment industry. Her journey is a powerful reminder of the transformative power of comedy and its ability to foster dialogue, challenge societal norms, and promote inclusivity. As she continues to evolve as both a performer and an activist, Szubanski's legacy in the comedy world remains firmly established, inspiring countless individuals to embrace their authentic selves and advocate for equality.

Chapter 2: Finding Her Voice

Discovering personal identity and sexuality

Journey of self-acceptance and coming out

The journey of self-acceptance and coming out is a deeply personal and often tumultuous process for many LGBTQ individuals, including Magda Szubanski. It involves a complex interplay of personal identity, societal expectations, and the quest for authenticity. According to [?], the coming out process can be understood through a series of stages, which include identity confusion, identity comparison, identity tolerance, identity acceptance, and ultimately, identity pride. Each stage presents unique challenges and opportunities for growth.

Identity Confusion

For Magda, the early stages of her life were marked by confusion regarding her sexual orientation. Growing up in a multicultural society, she faced the dual challenge of reconciling her Polish heritage with her emerging identity as a queer woman. This confusion is not uncommon; many LGBTQ individuals experience a sense of dissonance between their authentic selves and the identities imposed upon them by family and society.

$$\text{Identity Conflict} = \text{Societal Expectations} - \text{Personal Truth} \qquad (20)$$

This equation illustrates the tension between societal expectations and personal truth that many LGBTQ individuals face. The greater the societal pressure, the more pronounced the identity conflict becomes.

Identity Comparison and Tolerance

As Magda began to explore her sexual orientation, she entered the stage of identity comparison. This phase often involves comparing oneself to others within the LGBTQ community and grappling with feelings of isolation and fear. For Magda, the fear of rejection from her family and friends loomed large, a common concern among those contemplating coming out.

[?] discusses the concept of *minority stress*, which refers to the chronic stress experienced by marginalized groups due to their social status. This stress can manifest in various ways, including anxiety, depression, and low self-esteem. Magda's journey was not without its mental health challenges, as she navigated the societal stigma surrounding LGBTQ identities.

Identity Acceptance

The turning point in Magda's journey came with her growing self-acceptance. This phase is characterized by embracing one's identity and finding a community of support. For many, including Magda, this acceptance is often catalyzed by positive role models and representation in media.

Magda's comedic influences, such as Monty Python, not only shaped her comedic style but also provided a lens through which she could view her own experiences with humor and resilience. The transformative power of comedy allowed her to navigate her identity with a sense of empowerment, using laughter as a tool for self-acceptance.

$$\text{Self-Acceptance} = \text{Community Support} + \text{Positive Representation} \qquad (21)$$

This equation highlights the importance of community and representation in fostering self-acceptance. As Magda found her voice in the comedy scene, she began to embrace her identity more fully.

Coming Out

Coming out is often seen as a singular event, but it is, in reality, a continuous process that can occur multiple times in various contexts. For Magda, the act of coming out was both liberating and fraught with anxiety. The decision to publicly identify as a queer woman was a significant moment in her life, marked by both fear of rejection and hope for acceptance.

One notable instance of her coming out was during an interview where she candidly discussed her sexuality. This moment resonated with many in the LGBTQ community, as it demonstrated the courage required to live authentically.

$$\text{Coming Out} = \text{Authenticity} + \text{Risk of Rejection} \qquad (22)$$

This equation encapsulates the dual nature of coming out, where the desire for authenticity is often accompanied by the risk of rejection from loved ones and society.

The Impact of Coming Out

Magda's journey of self-acceptance and coming out not only transformed her personal life but also had a profound impact on her career. By embracing her identity, she became a trailblazer for LGBTQ representation in media, using her platform to advocate for equality and acceptance.

Her comedic work often included themes of identity and belonging, resonating with audiences and fostering a sense of community among those who felt marginalized. Through her humor, Magda was able to challenge stereotypes and promote understanding, illustrating the powerful role that comedy can play in social change.

In conclusion, Magda Szubanski's journey of self-acceptance and coming out reflects a broader narrative of resilience and empowerment within the LGBTQ community. Her experiences underscore the importance of authenticity, support, and representation in the ongoing fight for equality. As she continues to advocate for LGBTQ rights, her story serves as an inspiration for future generations, reminding us that the journey to self-acceptance is both personal and universal.

Impact on personal and professional relationships

The journey of self-acceptance and coming out is a deeply personal experience that can significantly influence both personal and professional relationships. For Magda Szubanski, this journey was characterized by both challenges and transformative moments that shaped her interactions with family, friends, colleagues, and the broader community.

Personal Relationships

Coming out often leads to a reevaluation of personal relationships. For many LGBTQ individuals, including Szubanski, the process can be fraught with anxiety about rejection or acceptance from loved ones. Szubanski's experience illustrates this dynamic, as she navigated the complexities of revealing her identity to her family. Research indicates that acceptance from family members is a crucial factor in the mental health and well-being of LGBTQ individuals. A study by Ryan et al. (2010) found that supportive family environments significantly reduce the risk of mental health issues among LGBTQ youth.

$$\text{Mental Health} \propto \text{Family Support} \qquad (23)$$

In Szubanski's case, her family's reaction was a mixture of support and confusion, illustrating the duality of acceptance and challenge. This reaction not only affected her emotional well-being but also influenced her subsequent relationships, as she learned to navigate the complexities of acceptance and rejection within her familial structure.

Friendships and Social Circles

As she embraced her identity, Szubanski's friendships evolved. The LGBTQ community often serves as a vital support network for individuals coming out, providing a sense of belonging and understanding that may be lacking in other areas of their lives. Szubanski found solace and solidarity within this community, which allowed her to forge deeper connections with like-minded individuals who shared similar struggles and triumphs.

However, the process of coming out can also lead to the loss of friendships, particularly if those in her social circle held homophobic views. Szubanski's experience underscores the notion that friendships can be tested during this period, as individuals confront their own biases and beliefs. A study by Herek (2009) highlights that social rejection can significantly impact the mental health of LGBTQ individuals, leading to feelings of isolation and loneliness.

$$\text{Social Acceptance} \propto \text{Mental Well-being} \qquad (24)$$

Szubanski's ability to cultivate supportive friendships within the LGBTQ community not only enriched her personal life but also provided her with a platform to engage in activism, demonstrating the interconnectedness of personal relationships and advocacy.

Professional Relationships

Szubanski's coming out had profound implications for her professional life as well. As a comedian and public figure, she faced the unique challenge of balancing her career aspirations with her desire to be authentic. The entertainment industry has historically been a mixed bag for LGBTQ individuals, often oscillating between acceptance and discrimination. Szubanski's decision to come out publicly positioned her as a trailblazer in the industry, paving the way for greater visibility and representation of LGBTQ individuals in media.

Her openness about her sexuality allowed her to connect with audiences on a deeper level, as many found her story relatable and inspiring. This connection is supported by the theory of social identity, which posits that individuals derive a sense of self from their group memberships, including sexual orientation. Szubanski's visibility as a queer comedian not only resonated with LGBTQ audiences but also educated and influenced heterosexual audiences, fostering a greater understanding of LGBTQ issues.

$$\text{Audience Connection} \propto \text{Authenticity} \qquad (25)$$

However, coming out also posed risks for Szubanski's career. The fear of backlash from conservative audiences or industry gatekeepers could potentially jeopardize her professional opportunities. Despite these challenges, Szubanski's commitment to authenticity ultimately strengthened her brand, as audiences increasingly valued transparency and vulnerability in public figures.

Navigating Challenges

The interplay between personal and professional relationships during Szubanski's coming out journey highlights the broader societal challenges faced by LGBTQ individuals. The stigma surrounding sexual orientation can lead to significant stress, affecting not only personal well-being but also professional dynamics. Szubanski's story serves as a reminder of the importance of creating inclusive environments where individuals can express their identities without fear of discrimination or retribution.

In summary, the impact of coming out on personal and professional relationships is multifaceted, characterized by both challenges and opportunities. Szubanski's journey reflects the broader LGBTQ experience, demonstrating the resilience required to navigate these complexities. Her ability to foster supportive relationships within her community and advocate for LGBTQ rights has not only enriched her life but also inspired countless others to embrace their identities and fight for equality.

$$\text{Resilience} = \text{Support} + \text{Authenticity} \qquad (26)$$

Entering the LGBTQ advocacy scene

Involvement with LGBTQ organizations and initiatives

Magda Szubanski's journey into the realm of LGBTQ advocacy began with a profound realization of her own identity and the pressing need for representation and rights within the community. Her involvement with various LGBTQ organizations and initiatives has not only been a personal mission but also a pivotal part of her career as a comedian and activist. This section explores the significant roles she has played in these organizations, the initiatives she has supported, and the broader implications of her work in the fight for equality.

Early Engagement with LGBTQ Organizations

Szubanski's engagement with LGBTQ organizations started in the early 2000s when she began to publicly embrace her identity. One of her first involvements was with the *Australian Coalition for Equality (ACE)*, an organization dedicated to advocating for same-sex marriage rights. Szubanski's participation in ACE was instrumental in mobilizing public support and raising awareness about the challenges faced by LGBTQ individuals in Australia. Her visibility as a public figure lent credibility and urgency to the cause, encouraging others to join the movement.

Using Comedy as a Platform for Advocacy

Szubanski recognized that comedy could serve as a powerful tool for social change. By leveraging her comedic talent, she has been able to address serious issues surrounding LGBTQ rights in a manner that resonates with a broad audience. For instance, her participation in events like the *Sydney Gay and Lesbian Mardi Gras* has allowed her to use humor to challenge stereotypes and promote acceptance. Szubanski's comedic performances often incorporate themes of identity, love, and equality, making complex issues more accessible to the general public.

Collaborative Initiatives

Throughout her advocacy career, Szubanski has collaborated with various organizations to amplify LGBTQ voices. One notable example is her work with *Twenty10*, a community organization that supports LGBTQ youth. By participating in fundraising events and awareness campaigns, Szubanski has helped to provide resources and support for young people grappling with their identities.

Her involvement has not only raised funds but has also fostered a sense of community and belonging among LGBTQ youth, highlighting the importance of support networks.

Advocacy for Anti-Discrimination Laws

Szubanski's activism extends beyond marriage equality; she has been a vocal advocate for comprehensive anti-discrimination laws. Her collaboration with organizations such as *Equality Australia* has focused on creating legislative changes that protect LGBTQ individuals from discrimination in various sectors, including employment, housing, and healthcare. Szubanski's efforts include public speaking engagements, media appearances, and direct lobbying of government officials. The impact of her advocacy is evident in the growing public discourse around LGBTQ rights and the eventual legislative changes that have occurred in Australia.

Addressing Mental Health Issues

In addition to her work on legal rights, Szubanski has been a passionate advocate for mental health support within the LGBTQ community. Recognizing the unique challenges faced by LGBTQ individuals, particularly youth, she has partnered with organizations like *Headspace* to promote mental health awareness. Szubanski has used her platform to speak openly about her own struggles with mental health, thereby destigmatizing these issues and encouraging others to seek help. This aspect of her advocacy is crucial, as LGBTQ individuals often face higher rates of mental health challenges due to societal discrimination and isolation.

Impact on Public Perception

Szubanski's involvement with LGBTQ organizations has significantly influenced public perception of LGBTQ issues in Australia. Through her advocacy, she has contributed to a cultural shift that increasingly embraces diversity and inclusion. Her presence in the media and her outspoken nature have helped to humanize the struggles faced by LGBTQ individuals, fostering empathy and understanding among the broader population. This change in public sentiment is reflected in the growing support for LGBTQ rights, including marriage equality, which was achieved in Australia in 2017.

Conclusion

Magda Szubanski's involvement with LGBTQ organizations and initiatives exemplifies the power of advocacy rooted in personal experience and public visibility. Through her comedic talents, collaborative efforts, and commitment to social justice, she has made a lasting impact on the LGBTQ rights movement in Australia. Her journey underscores the importance of representation and the role that individuals can play in shaping societal attitudes towards equality and acceptance. As she continues her work, Szubanski remains a beacon of hope and inspiration for future generations of LGBTQ activists.

Using comedy as a tool for social change

Comedy has long been recognized not only as a form of entertainment but also as a powerful medium for social commentary and change. Magda Szubanski, through her unique blend of humor and activism, has harnessed the comedic arts to challenge societal norms and foster a more inclusive environment for LGBTQ individuals. This section delves into the theories surrounding comedy as a catalyst for social change, the problems it addresses, and the practical examples of its effectiveness in advocating for LGBTQ rights.

Theoretical Framework

The relationship between comedy and social change can be understood through several theoretical lenses. One prominent theory is the **Incongruity Theory**, which posits that humor arises from the perception of incongruities between expectations and reality. When comedians highlight societal absurdities—such as homophobia or discrimination—they prompt audiences to confront uncomfortable truths while simultaneously eliciting laughter. This cognitive dissonance can lead to a reevaluation of preconceived notions and biases.

Another relevant theory is the **Relief Theory**, which suggests that humor serves as a coping mechanism that allows individuals to release tension surrounding taboo subjects. By addressing LGBTQ issues through comedy, comedians like Szubanski provide a safe space for audiences to engage with difficult topics, ultimately fostering understanding and empathy. This approach can be particularly effective in breaking down barriers and initiating conversations about acceptance and equality.

Challenges in Using Comedy for Advocacy

While comedy can be a potent tool for social change, it is not without its challenges. One significant problem is the risk of **misinterpretation**. Jokes about sensitive subjects can easily be taken out of context or misread, leading to backlash or reinforcing harmful stereotypes. Szubanski herself has navigated this treacherous terrain, often facing criticism for her bold comedic choices. This highlights the importance of context and intention in comedic discourse.

Moreover, there is the challenge of **audience reception**. Different demographics may respond to humor in varied ways based on their cultural backgrounds, personal experiences, and levels of awareness regarding LGBTQ issues. Szubanski has adeptly tailored her material to resonate with diverse audiences, often using relatable anecdotes and universal themes to bridge gaps in understanding.

Examples of Comedy as Advocacy

Szubanski's comedic work serves as a prime example of how humor can be leveraged for advocacy. One notable instance is her participation in the **Yes Campaign** for marriage equality in Australia. Through her platform, she utilized humor to humanize the fight for LGBTQ rights, sharing personal stories that resonated with both supporters and skeptics alike. Her appearance on television shows, where she infused humor into serious discussions about marriage equality, helped to shift public opinion and normalize conversations about LGBTQ relationships.

Additionally, Szubanski's comedic performances often include **satirical elements** that critique societal norms. For instance, her portrayal of characters who challenge heteronormative expectations serves to expose the absurdity of rigid gender roles and stereotypes. By using laughter to highlight these issues, she encourages audiences to question their own biases and consider alternative perspectives.

The Impact of Humor on Social Change

The effectiveness of comedy in driving social change is evidenced by its ability to foster dialogue and create a sense of community among marginalized groups. Szubanski's work has not only entertained but also empowered countless individuals within the LGBTQ community. Her humor resonates with those who have faced discrimination, offering a sense of solidarity and validation.

Moreover, comedy can serve as a bridge between opposing viewpoints. By presenting LGBTQ issues in a humorous light, Szubanski has been able to engage audiences who may otherwise be resistant to discussions about equality. This approach exemplifies the potential of comedy to transcend barriers and promote understanding in a divided society.

In conclusion, Magda Szubanski's use of comedy as a tool for social change underscores the profound impact that humor can have in advocating for LGBTQ rights. Through her innovative approach, she has demonstrated that laughter can be a powerful vehicle for challenging societal norms, fostering empathy, and inspiring action. As the landscape of LGBTQ activism continues to evolve, the role of comedy remains a vital component in the ongoing fight for equality and acceptance.

Speaking out against discrimination

Fearless and unapologetic activism

Magda Szubanski's journey as an LGBTQ activist is marked by her fearless and unapologetic approach to challenging societal norms and advocating for equality. Her activism is rooted in a deep understanding of the complexities surrounding LGBTQ issues, informed by both personal experiences and a commitment to social justice. This section explores the theoretical underpinnings of her activism, the problems she confronts, and the examples that illustrate her bold stance.

Theoretical Framework

At the core of Szubanski's activism lies the theory of **intersectionality**, coined by Kimberlé Crenshaw in 1989. Intersectionality posits that individuals experience overlapping systems of discrimination based on various identity factors, including race, gender, sexuality, and class. Szubanski's advocacy is a testament to this theory; she recognizes that LGBTQ rights cannot be viewed in isolation but rather must be understood within the broader context of social justice.

Szubanski's work also reflects the principles of **queer theory**, which challenges the binary understanding of gender and sexuality. Queer theory emphasizes fluidity and the rejection of normative frameworks, allowing for a more inclusive understanding of identity. By embracing her own queerness and challenging societal expectations, Szubanski embodies the essence of queer activism, encouraging others to do the same.

Confronting Societal Problems

Szubanski's activism addresses several pressing issues within the LGBTQ community. One of the most significant problems she confronts is **homophobia**, which manifests in various forms, including discrimination, violence, and systemic inequality. Her unapologetic stance is particularly crucial in a society where LGBTQ individuals often face marginalization.

For instance, the Australian Marriage Law Postal Survey in 2017 highlighted the pervasive homophobia in public discourse. Szubanski used her platform to advocate for marriage equality, leveraging her comedic talent to engage a broader audience. She confronted anti-LGBTQ rhetoric head-on, challenging the narratives that sought to dehumanize LGBTQ individuals. Her viral social media posts and public appearances became rallying cries for change, demonstrating that humor can be a powerful tool in activism.

Examples of Fearless Activism

Szubanski's activism is replete with examples of her fearless approach. One notable instance occurred during a live television interview in 2015, where she passionately spoke out against the government's treatment of LGBTQ youth. Her emotional appeal resonated with viewers, drawing attention to the mental health crisis faced by young LGBTQ individuals. Szubanski's willingness to share her own struggles with mental health further humanized the issue, fostering empathy and understanding.

Another example of her unapologetic activism is her involvement in the **Wear It Purple Day** campaign, which aims to support LGBTQ youth. Szubanski has consistently used her platform to promote this initiative, encouraging people to wear purple as a symbol of solidarity. Her participation not only raises awareness but also sends a message that LGBTQ youth deserve to be seen and heard. By standing alongside these young individuals, Szubanski exemplifies the importance of allyship in activism.

Challenging Normative Constructs

Szubanski's activism also challenges normative constructs surrounding gender and sexuality. In her comedy, she often subverts traditional gender roles, using humor to critique societal expectations. This approach not only entertains but also provokes thought, encouraging audiences to question their own beliefs about gender and sexuality.

For example, in her stand-up routines, Szubanski often addresses the absurdities of heteronormative culture, highlighting the limitations it imposes on individuals.

By using comedy as a vehicle for social commentary, she creates a space for dialogue and reflection, inviting audiences to reconsider their perspectives on LGBTQ issues.

The Impact of Fearless Activism

The impact of Szubanski's fearless activism extends beyond individual anecdotes; it contributes to a larger cultural shift towards acceptance and equality. Her unapologetic approach has inspired countless individuals to embrace their identities and advocate for their rights. By publicly challenging discrimination, Szubanski empowers others to do the same, fostering a sense of community and solidarity within the LGBTQ movement.

Moreover, her activism has garnered recognition and respect within the entertainment industry. Szubanski's willingness to speak out has paved the way for more inclusive representations of LGBTQ individuals in media. As a result, her impact transcends her own career, influencing a generation of artists and activists who seek to amplify LGBTQ voices.

Conclusion

In conclusion, Magda Szubanski's fearless and unapologetic activism serves as a powerful example of how individuals can challenge societal norms and advocate for LGBTQ rights. Grounded in theories of intersectionality and queer theory, her work addresses critical issues such as homophobia and mental health, while also challenging normative constructs surrounding gender and sexuality. Through her bold stance and commitment to social justice, Szubanski has left an indelible mark on the LGBTQ movement, inspiring others to embrace their identities and fight for equality. Her legacy is a testament to the power of activism rooted in authenticity and courage.

Challenging homophobic attitudes in society

In the realm of LGBTQ activism, challenging homophobic attitudes is a critical endeavor that requires both courage and strategy. Magda Szubanski, as a prominent figure in Australian comedy and activism, has utilized her platform to confront these pervasive attitudes head-on. This section explores the theoretical frameworks surrounding homophobia, the societal problems it engenders, and the examples of Szubanski's impactful interventions.

Theoretical Frameworks

Homophobia can be understood through various theoretical lenses. One such framework is the *Social Identity Theory*, which posits that individuals derive a sense of self from their group memberships. When people perceive their social identity as threatened, they may react defensively, leading to discriminatory behaviors against those perceived as different. This theory elucidates why individuals may harbor negative attitudes towards LGBTQ individuals; it stems from a perceived threat to their own identity and societal norms.

Additionally, the *Heteronormativity Theory* provides insight into how societal structures privilege heterosexual relationships while marginalizing others. Heteronormativity reinforces the idea that heterosexuality is the default or "normal" sexual orientation, which can result in systemic discrimination against LGBTQ individuals. Understanding these frameworks is crucial for activists like Szubanski, who aim to dismantle these ingrained biases.

Societal Problems Stemming from Homophobia

Homophobic attitudes manifest in various detrimental ways, affecting both individuals and communities. One significant issue is the prevalence of *mental health problems* among LGBTQ individuals, often exacerbated by societal rejection and discrimination. Studies have shown that LGBTQ youth are at a higher risk of depression, anxiety, and suicidal ideation compared to their heterosexual peers. Szubanski's advocacy often highlights these alarming statistics, emphasizing the urgent need for societal change.

Moreover, homophobia contributes to the perpetuation of *violence and hate crimes* against LGBTQ individuals. According to reports from organizations such as the Australian Human Rights Commission, hate crimes based on sexual orientation remain a pressing concern. Szubanski has used her comedic platform to address these issues, blending humor with poignant commentary to raise awareness and foster empathy.

Examples of Szubanski's Interventions

Magda Szubanski's approach to challenging homophobic attitudes is characterized by her fearless and unapologetic stance. One notable example is her involvement in the campaign for marriage equality in Australia. During this time, Szubanski leveraged her celebrity status to amplify the voices of LGBTQ individuals, sharing personal stories that resonated with the public. Her heartfelt video messages and public appearances were instrumental in shifting public opinion, demonstrating the power of personal narratives in combating prejudice.

Another example is her participation in the *"Yes"* campaign, which sought to promote acceptance of same-sex marriage. Szubanski's candid discussions about her own experiences as a gay woman served to humanize the issue, challenging the often abstract and dehumanizing rhetoric used by opponents of marriage equality. She effectively utilized social media platforms to reach a broader audience, creating a dialogue that encouraged understanding and compassion.

Furthermore, Szubanski has not shied away from addressing homophobic remarks directly. In various interviews and public forums, she has confronted individuals who perpetuate harmful stereotypes, employing humor as a tool to disarm hostility. This tactic not only highlights the absurdity of homophobic attitudes but also fosters a more inclusive conversation.

Conclusion

Challenging homophobic attitudes in society is a multifaceted endeavor that requires a deep understanding of the underlying theories, recognition of the societal problems at play, and the courage to confront these issues head-on. Through her activism, Magda Szubanski exemplifies how humor, personal storytelling, and direct confrontation can serve as powerful tools in the fight against homophobia. By continuing to challenge societal norms and advocate for LGBTQ rights, Szubanski inspires others to join the movement towards a more inclusive and equitable society.

Trailblazing LGBTQ representations in the media

Breaking stereotypes and paving the way for others

Magda Szubanski's journey in the entertainment industry has been marked by her relentless commitment to breaking stereotypes and championing LGBTQ representation. As a prominent figure in Australian comedy, she has utilized her platform to challenge conventional narratives surrounding gender and sexuality, paving the way for a more inclusive media landscape.

Challenging Norms through Comedy

Comedy has long served as a vehicle for social commentary, allowing artists to address sensitive issues in a manner that resonates with audiences. Szubanski's unique comedic style blends humor with poignant insights, often drawing from her own experiences as a queer woman. By incorporating her identity into her performances, she not only entertains but also educates her audience about the complexities of LGBTQ life.

For instance, in her iconic role as Sharon Strzelecki on the television show *Kath & Kim*, Szubanski portrayed a character that defied traditional feminine stereotypes. Sharon was not only unapologetically herself but also a representation of the diversity within the LGBTQ community. This portrayal challenged the often one-dimensional representations of queer characters in mainstream media, which frequently leaned towards hypersexualization or tragic narratives. Instead, Sharon was relatable, humorous, and multifaceted, allowing viewers to see LGBTQ individuals as integral members of society rather than mere caricatures.

Visibility and Representation

Szubanski's visibility as an openly queer comedian has contributed significantly to the representation of LGBTQ individuals in Australian media. According to the *Media, Diversity and Social Change Initiative*, representation matters; when marginalized groups see themselves reflected in media, it fosters a sense of belonging and acceptance. Szubanski's presence in the entertainment industry has inspired countless individuals to embrace their identities and pursue careers in creative fields.

Moreover, her willingness to speak candidly about her experiences has encouraged other LGBTQ artists to share their stories. This ripple effect is vital in dismantling stereotypes, as it showcases the diversity of experiences within the LGBTQ community. Szubanski's advocacy extends beyond her performances; she actively engages in discussions around representation, emphasizing the need for authentic portrayals of queer lives in all forms of media.

Empowering Future Generations

Szubanski's impact is not limited to her own career; she has taken on the role of mentor and advocate for emerging LGBTQ talent. By using her platform to promote and uplift other queer voices, she is actively shaping the next generation of artists. Initiatives such as the *LGBTQ+ Arts and Culture Fund* aim to provide resources and support for young creatives, ensuring that they have the tools necessary to succeed in an industry that has historically marginalized their stories.

Furthermore, Szubanski's involvement in campaigns like the *YES* campaign for marriage equality highlights her commitment to fighting for the rights of LGBTQ individuals. By standing at the forefront of these movements, she not only challenges societal norms but also encourages others to join the fight for equality. The visibility of LGBTQ activists in mainstream media plays a crucial role in normalizing queer identities and fostering acceptance.

Theoretical Perspectives on Stereotype Breaking

From a theoretical standpoint, the work of Szubanski can be analyzed through the lens of Judith Butler's concept of gender performativity. Butler posits that gender is not a fixed identity but rather a series of performances that are socially constructed. Szubanski's performances challenge the rigid binaries of gender and sexuality, illustrating the fluidity of identity. By embodying various roles that defy traditional expectations, she invites audiences to reconsider their perceptions of gender norms.

Additionally, the *Social Identity Theory* suggests that individuals derive a sense of self from their group memberships. Szubanski's visibility as a queer comedian allows LGBTQ individuals to see themselves represented in a positive light, fostering pride and solidarity within the community. Her work helps to dismantle the stigma associated with being queer, encouraging acceptance and understanding.

Conclusion

In conclusion, Magda Szubanski's contributions to breaking stereotypes and paving the way for others in the LGBTQ community are profound. Through her comedic brilliance, advocacy, and unwavering commitment to representation, she has not only transformed the landscape of Australian media but has also inspired a generation of activists and artists. As society continues to grapple with issues of identity and acceptance, Szubanski's legacy serves as a beacon of hope, reminding us of the power of visibility and the importance of authentic storytelling in the fight for equality.

Positive impact on LGBTQ visibility and acceptance

The journey towards LGBTQ visibility and acceptance has been a complex and multifaceted process, marked by both triumphs and ongoing challenges. Magda Szubanski's contributions to this movement serve as a powerful testament to the influence that media representation can have on societal attitudes and perceptions. Through her work, she has not only entertained audiences but has also sparked critical conversations about identity, acceptance, and the importance of visibility for marginalized communities.

Theoretical Framework

To understand the impact of Szubanski's work on LGBTQ visibility, we can draw on several theoretical frameworks, including social identity theory and the theory of representation. Social identity theory posits that individuals derive part of their self-concept from their membership in social groups, including those defined by sexual orientation. This theory suggests that positive representation in media can enhance the self-esteem and social identity of LGBTQ individuals, fostering a sense of belonging and acceptance within society.

The theory of representation, as articulated by Stuart Hall, emphasizes that the way groups are portrayed in media can significantly influence public perceptions and attitudes. Hall argues that representation is not merely about reflecting reality but actively shapes it. Therefore, Szubanski's roles in popular television shows and her public persona have played a critical role in challenging stereotypes and fostering a more nuanced understanding of LGBTQ identities.

Breaking Stereotypes

One of the most significant ways in which Szubanski has positively impacted LGBTQ visibility is through her ability to break down harmful stereotypes. Traditionally, LGBTQ characters in media were often relegated to caricatures or tragic figures, reinforcing negative perceptions. Szubanski, however, has portrayed complex, relatable characters that resonate with audiences on a personal level. For example, her role as Sharon Strzelecki in the hit television series *Kath & Kim* presents a character who is unapologetically herself—funny, quirky, and deeply human.

This representation challenges the notion that LGBTQ individuals must conform to specific societal expectations or norms. By embodying a character who embraces her uniqueness, Szubanski provides a model for acceptance and self-love, encouraging viewers to celebrate their own identities. The laughter and joy that her character brings to the screen serve as a counter-narrative to the often somber depictions of LGBTQ lives.

Increasing Visibility

Szubanski's visibility as a public figure has also played a crucial role in normalizing LGBTQ identities in Australian society. Her candidness about her own sexuality and experiences has opened the door for conversations about LGBTQ issues in mainstream discourse. In 2012, Szubanski publicly came out as gay during a campaign for marriage equality, an act that not only affirmed her identity but also inspired others to embrace their truth.

The impact of such visibility cannot be overstated. Research indicates that increased visibility of LGBTQ individuals in media correlates with greater acceptance and support from the broader community. For instance, a study conducted by the *Pew Research Center* found that individuals who consume LGBTQ-inclusive media are more likely to support LGBTQ rights and express positive attitudes towards LGBTQ individuals. Szubanski's presence in the media landscape has thus contributed to a gradual shift in societal attitudes, fostering a culture of acceptance and understanding.

Advocacy Through Humor

Humor has been a powerful tool in Szubanski's advocacy for LGBTQ visibility. By using comedy to address serious issues, she has created a space where difficult conversations can take place in a more approachable manner. This approach not only engages audiences but also disarms prejudices, allowing for a deeper exploration of LGBTQ issues.

For example, during her stand-up performances and television appearances, Szubanski often incorporates humor to highlight the absurdity of homophobia and discrimination. This strategy not only entertains but also educates, prompting audiences to reflect on their own beliefs and biases. The ability to laugh while confronting uncomfortable truths is a hallmark of Szubanski's style, making her a unique and effective advocate for LGBTQ rights.

Conclusion

In conclusion, Magda Szubanski's impact on LGBTQ visibility and acceptance is profound and multifaceted. Through her comedic talent, authentic representation, and fearless advocacy, she has contributed significantly to the normalization of LGBTQ identities in Australian culture. By breaking stereotypes, increasing visibility, and using humor as a tool for social change, Szubanski has not only influenced public perceptions but has also empowered countless individuals to embrace their identities. As we continue to navigate the complexities of LGBTQ rights and representation, her legacy serves as a beacon of hope and inspiration for future generations of activists and allies.

Balancing comedy and activism

Challenges and rewards of being an LGBTQ advocate

Being an LGBTQ advocate is a multifaceted journey filled with both challenges and rewards. This section delves into the complexities faced by advocates, highlighting the emotional, social, and political landscapes they navigate, while also celebrating the profound impact of their work.

Challenges Faced by LGBTQ Advocates

1. Societal Backlash One of the most significant challenges advocates face is societal backlash. This can manifest in various forms, including verbal harassment, physical violence, and systemic discrimination. For instance, during the campaign for marriage equality in Australia, many advocates received threats and faced intense scrutiny from conservative groups. The psychological toll of such backlash can lead to anxiety and depression among advocates, as they grapple with the fear of personal safety and societal rejection.

2. Emotional Labor Advocacy work often requires immense emotional labor. Advocates must constantly engage with painful narratives of discrimination and injustice, which can lead to burnout. The emotional toll is compounded by the need to remain resilient and optimistic in the face of adversity. Research by Hochschild (1983) on emotional labor highlights that individuals in service-oriented roles often suppress their emotions to maintain a facade of positivity, which can be exhausting over time. For LGBTQ advocates, this can mean putting on a brave face while internally struggling with despair over ongoing injustices.

3. Intersectionality and Inclusivity Another challenge is the need to address intersectionality within the LGBTQ community. Advocates must navigate the complexities of race, gender, socioeconomic status, and other identities that intersect with sexual orientation. For example, LGBTQ individuals of color often face compounded discrimination that may not be adequately addressed by mainstream LGBTQ advocacy. This necessitates a broader understanding and inclusivity within advocacy efforts, which can be difficult to achieve. The theory of intersectionality, as posited by Crenshaw (1989), emphasizes the importance of recognizing how overlapping identities impact individuals' experiences, thus complicating advocacy efforts.

4.   Funding and Resources   Securing funding and resources for LGBTQ advocacy can also pose significant challenges.   Many organizations rely on donations and grants, which can be inconsistent. This financial instability can limit the scope of advocacy work and hinder the ability to create impactful programs. For instance, during economic downturns, LGBTQ organizations often face cuts in funding, which can lead to reduced services for marginalized communities.

Rewards of Being an LGBTQ Advocate

1. Fostering Change   Despite the challenges, one of the most rewarding aspects of being an LGBTQ advocate is the ability to foster meaningful change. Advocates play a crucial role in shaping public policy and societal attitudes. For example, the tireless work of advocates during the marriage equality campaign in Australia led to the historic legalization of same-sex marriage in 2017. This achievement not only represented a significant legal victory but also symbolized a shift in societal acceptance of LGBTQ individuals.

2.   Building Community   Advocacy also provides opportunities for building strong, supportive communities. LGBTQ advocates often find camaraderie among like-minded individuals who share similar experiences and goals. This sense of belonging can be incredibly empowering and serve as a source of strength. Community events, pride parades, and advocacy meetings create spaces for individuals to connect, share their stories, and support one another, fostering resilience in the face of adversity.

3.   Personal Growth and Empowerment   Engaging in advocacy can lead to profound personal growth.   Advocates often develop skills in public speaking, leadership, and critical thinking, which can enhance their professional and personal lives. The act of standing up for one's beliefs can also foster a deep sense of empowerment.   As noted by Freire (1970), the process of critical consciousness—where individuals recognize and challenge oppressive structures—can lead to transformative social action and personal liberation.

4. Leaving a Legacy   Finally, the work of LGBTQ advocates contributes to a lasting legacy of progress and acceptance.   By fighting for equality and justice, advocates pave the way for future generations to live authentically and without fear. The stories of activists, such as Magda Szubanski, inspire young LGBTQ individuals to embrace their identities and engage in advocacy themselves.   This cyclical nature of activism ensures that the fight for equality continues, creating a ripple effect of change.

Conclusion

In conclusion, while the challenges of being an LGBTQ advocate can be daunting, the rewards are equally significant. Advocates like Magda Szubanski exemplify the resilience and determination needed to effect change in society. By navigating the complexities of advocacy with courage and compassion, they not only fight for their rights but also inspire others to join the movement, ultimately contributing to a more inclusive and equitable world.

Bibliography

[1] Hochschild, A. R. (1983). *The Managed Heart: Commercialization of Human Feeling*. University of California Press.

[2] Crenshaw, K. (1989). Demarginalizing the Intersection of Race and Sex: A Black Feminist Critique of Antidiscrimination Doctrine, Feminist Theory and Antiracist Politics. *University of Chicago Legal Forum*, 1989(1), 139-167.

[3] Freire, P. (1970). *Pedagogy of the Oppressed*. Continuum.

Harnessing humor to convey important messages

Humor has long been recognized as a powerful tool for social change, particularly in the realm of LGBTQ activism. By employing wit and satire, activists like Magda Szubanski have been able to address serious issues while simultaneously engaging and entertaining their audiences. This section explores the theoretical underpinnings of humor in activism, the challenges faced, and the effective strategies utilized by Szubanski in her advocacy.

Theoretical Framework

The use of humor in activism can be understood through several theoretical lenses, including the Incongruity Theory and the Superiority Theory. Incongruity Theory posits that humor arises when there is a discrepancy between what is expected and what actually occurs. This can be particularly effective in activism, as it allows for the subversion of dominant narratives and the highlighting of societal absurdities. For instance, Szubanski often juxtaposes the serious nature of LGBTQ rights with humorous anecdotes, creating a cognitive dissonance that prompts audiences to reconsider their views.

Conversely, Superiority Theory suggests that humor derives from the feeling of superiority over others, often at their expense. While this can be problematic if it perpetuates stereotypes, when used thoughtfully, it can empower marginalized communities by reclaiming narratives. Szubanski's comedic style often involves self-deprecation and irony, allowing her to connect with her audience while simultaneously challenging societal norms.

Challenges in Utilizing Humor

Despite its effectiveness, harnessing humor in activism is not without its challenges. One major issue is the risk of trivializing serious topics. Activists must carefully balance humor with the gravity of the issues at hand. For example, while making jokes about discrimination can be a way to cope and foster resilience, it can also lead to perceptions that the struggle for rights is not serious or urgent.

Moreover, humor is subjective; what one person finds funny, another may find offensive. This variability can lead to backlash and alienation within the very communities activists aim to support. Szubanski, for instance, has faced criticism for jokes that some perceived as inappropriate or insensitive. Navigating this landscape requires a deep understanding of audience dynamics and cultural contexts.

Effective Strategies Employed by Szubanski

Magda Szubanski has effectively harnessed humor to convey important messages through several strategies:

- **Storytelling:** Szubanski often uses personal narratives to illustrate broader societal issues. By sharing her own experiences of coming out and facing discrimination, she creates a relatable context that resonates with her audience. This approach not only entertains but also educates, fostering empathy and understanding.

- **Satire and Parody:** Szubanski employs satire to critique homophobic attitudes and policies. By exaggerating these viewpoints in a humorous light, she exposes their absurdity. For example, her comedic sketches often mimic outdated stereotypes, thereby dismantling them while eliciting laughter.

- **Engaging with Current Events:** Szubanski's ability to weave humor into discussions about contemporary issues, such as marriage equality, allows her to remain relevant and impactful. By addressing these topics in a light-hearted manner, she captures the attention of a broader audience, making complex issues more accessible.

◆ **Collaborative Humor:** Szubanski frequently collaborates with other comedians and activists, creating a collective comedic voice that amplifies LGBTQ messages. This collaboration not only strengthens community ties but also diversifies the humor presented, appealing to a wider audience.

Examples of Impactful Humor

One notable example of Szubanski's use of humor to address LGBTQ issues occurred during her public support for marriage equality in Australia. In a television appearance, she humorously recounted her own experiences with love and relationships, juxtaposing them with the legal barriers faced by same-sex couples. This approach not only humanized the issue but also made it relatable to viewers who may not have previously engaged with LGBTQ rights.

Another example is her use of social media, where she often shares humorous memes and videos that challenge homophobic rhetoric. By responding to negative comments with wit, she not only disarms her critics but also encourages her followers to engage in constructive dialogue about LGBTQ rights.

Conclusion

In conclusion, harnessing humor to convey important messages is a potent strategy in LGBTQ activism, as exemplified by Magda Szubanski. While challenges exist, the effective use of humor can educate, engage, and inspire audiences to reconsider their views on critical issues. By blending comedy with activism, Szubanski has not only entertained but also paved the way for meaningful conversations about equality and acceptance. As the landscape of LGBTQ rights continues to evolve, the role of humor in activism remains an invaluable asset in the fight for social justice.

Chapter 3: Standing Up for Equality

Fight for marriage equality

Campaigning for same-sex marriage rights

The fight for same-sex marriage rights in Australia has been a pivotal chapter in the ongoing struggle for LGBTQ equality. At the forefront of this movement was Magda Szubanski, whose passionate advocacy and unique ability to engage the public through humor played a significant role in shaping the discourse around marriage equality.

The campaign for same-sex marriage in Australia gained momentum in the early 2000s, paralleling similar movements worldwide. The historical context reveals a landscape fraught with challenges, including entrenched homophobia and political resistance. Despite these obstacles, activists mobilized to create a powerful coalition advocating for change.

Theoretical Framework

To understand the dynamics of the marriage equality movement, we can apply the *Social Movement Theory*, which posits that social movements arise in response to perceived injustices and seek to create social change through collective action. The theory emphasizes the importance of resources, political opportunities, and framing in the success of social movements.

In the case of same-sex marriage, the framing of the issue was critical. Advocates like Szubanski reframed marriage not merely as a legal contract but as a fundamental human right, emphasizing love, commitment, and family. This reframing helped shift public perception, making the argument for marriage equality more relatable and emotionally resonant.

Challenges Faced

Despite the compelling arguments for marriage equality, the campaign faced numerous challenges:

1.   **Political Resistance**: The Australian government had historically resisted calls for same-sex marriage. The 2004 amendment to the Marriage Act explicitly defined marriage as a union between a man and a woman, effectively sidelining LGBTQ couples. This legal barrier necessitated a concerted effort to advocate for legislative change.

2. **Public Opinion**: While support for same-sex marriage grew over time, significant portions of the population remained opposed. Activists had to navigate this landscape, using strategic communication to address misconceptions and fears surrounding LGBTQ relationships.

3. **Media Representation**: The portrayal of LGBTQ issues in the media often influenced public opinion. Szubanski's visibility in mainstream media allowed her to challenge stereotypes and humanize the struggle for marriage equality. Her comedic approach made the issue accessible, drawing in audiences who might otherwise remain indifferent.

Magda Szubanski's Role

Szubanski's involvement in the campaign was multifaceted. She leveraged her celebrity status to amplify the message of equality. Notably, her heartfelt public declaration of support during the 2017 postal survey on same-sex marriage resonated with many Australians. Szubanski utilized social media platforms to engage directly with the public, sharing personal stories and advocating for a "yes" vote.

$$\text{Support} = f(\text{Visibility, Personal Stories, Public Engagement}) \quad (27)$$

This equation illustrates that support for same-sex marriage is a function of visibility, personal narratives, and active public engagement—elements that Szubanski embodied throughout her advocacy.

Impact of the Campaign

The culmination of years of activism and public discourse led to the historic passage of the Marriage Amendment (Same-Sex Marriage) Act in December 2017. This legislative victory was not just a triumph for LGBTQ rights but a testament to the power of grassroots activism and the role of influential figures like Szubanski in changing hearts and minds.

The successful campaign for same-sex marriage in Australia serves as a model for other countries still grappling with similar issues. It demonstrates that through persistent advocacy, strategic framing, and the courage to share personal stories, significant social change is possible.

In conclusion, the campaign for same-sex marriage rights in Australia, championed by activists such as Magda Szubanski, exemplifies the intersection of humor, personal narrative, and political activism. The journey towards equality continues, but the achievements of the past serve as a beacon of hope and inspiration for future generations of activists.

Role in shaping public opinion through media

The media plays a crucial role in shaping public opinion, particularly regarding social issues such as LGBTQ rights. Magda Szubanski, through her comedic prowess and public persona, has effectively utilized various media platforms to influence societal perceptions and attitudes towards the LGBTQ community. This section will explore the theoretical frameworks surrounding media influence, the challenges faced in advocating for LGBTQ rights, and specific examples of Szubanski's impact.

Theoretical Frameworks

The influence of media on public opinion can be understood through several theoretical lenses, including the **Agenda-Setting Theory** and the **Framing Theory**.

- **Agenda-Setting Theory** posits that the media doesn't tell people what to think, but rather what to think about. By prioritizing certain issues, the media can shape the public discourse. Szubanski's visibility in the media has brought LGBTQ issues to the forefront, encouraging conversations that may have otherwise remained marginalized.

- **Framing Theory** suggests that the way information is presented influences how audiences interpret it. Szubanski's comedic framing of LGBTQ issues has allowed her to challenge stereotypes and promote empathy, making complex issues more relatable and digestible for the general public.

Challenges in Advocacy

Despite the potential of media to influence public opinion positively, LGBTQ advocates like Szubanski face significant challenges:

+ **Media Representation:** Historically, LGBTQ individuals have been underrepresented or misrepresented in media. Szubanski has fought against these stereotypes by presenting authentic narratives that resonate with both LGBTQ individuals and allies.

+ **Backlash and Criticism:** Advocating for LGBTQ rights in the media can attract backlash from conservative groups. Szubanski's fearless approach to addressing homophobia has sometimes resulted in personal attacks, yet she has remained undeterred, using her platform to amplify marginalized voices.

Examples of Impact

Magda Szubanski's influence on public opinion regarding LGBTQ rights is evident through various media appearances and initiatives:

+ **Television and Film:** Szubanski's roles in popular Australian television shows, such as *Kath & Kim*, have allowed her to normalize LGBTQ narratives within mainstream entertainment. Her character's experiences often reflect the struggles faced by LGBTQ individuals, fostering understanding and empathy among viewers.

+ **Social Media Engagement:** Szubanski has harnessed the power of social media to engage with her audience directly. Her candid discussions about her own experiences as a queer woman have humanized LGBTQ issues, encouraging followers to reflect on their own biases and attitudes.

+ **Public Campaigns:** Szubanski has actively participated in campaigns advocating for marriage equality, utilizing her media presence to mobilize support. Her involvement in the *Yes Campaign* for same-sex marriage in Australia showcased her ability to shape public opinion through strategic messaging and visibility.

Conclusion

In conclusion, Magda Szubanski's role in shaping public opinion through media exemplifies the powerful intersection of entertainment and activism. By leveraging her comedic talents and media presence, she has challenged societal norms, fostered dialogue, and significantly contributed to the advancement of LGBTQ rights in Australia. As media continues to evolve, the potential for advocates like Szubanski to influence public opinion remains a vital component in the ongoing fight for equality and acceptance.

Addressing other LGBTQ rights issues

Advocacy for anti-discrimination laws

The fight for anti-discrimination laws has been a cornerstone of LGBTQ activism, particularly in Australia, where the legal landscape has undergone significant transformation over the past few decades. Advocacy for these laws is not merely about legal recognition but also about the fundamental human rights of individuals to live authentically without fear of persecution or prejudice.

Theoretical Framework

The advocacy for anti-discrimination laws can be understood through the lens of several key theories, including social justice theory, human rights theory, and intersectionality. Social justice theory posits that all individuals are entitled to equal rights and opportunities, and discrimination based on sexual orientation or gender identity undermines this principle. Human rights theory emphasizes the inherent dignity and worth of every person, which is compromised when discriminatory practices are allowed to persist. Intersectionality, a term coined by Kimberlé Crenshaw, provides a framework for understanding how various forms of discrimination—such as those based on race, gender, and sexuality—intersect and compound the experiences of marginalized individuals.

Historical Context

Historically, Australia has seen a patchwork of laws regarding LGBTQ rights, with significant disparities between states and territories. The movement towards comprehensive anti-discrimination legislation began in earnest in the late 20th century, catalyzed by the activism of individuals and organizations who recognized the urgent need for legal protections. For instance, the introduction of the *Sex Discrimination Act 1984* marked a pivotal moment, as it prohibited discrimination on the basis of sex, marital status, and pregnancy. However, it did not initially include protections based on sexual orientation.

Key Advocacy Efforts

One of the most significant advocacy efforts for anti-discrimination laws in Australia has been led by organizations such as *Australian Marriage Equality* and *The Equality Campaign*. These groups have tirelessly worked to raise awareness about the importance of legal protections against discrimination. For example, the campaign for the inclusion of sexual orientation in anti-discrimination laws gained momentum in the early 2000s, leading to various state-level reforms.

In 2013, the *Australian Capital Territory* (ACT) passed its own same-sex marriage legislation, a move that was quickly challenged in the High Court. This case highlighted not only the legal complexities surrounding marriage equality but also the broader implications for anti-discrimination protections. The High Court's ruling ultimately reaffirmed the need for comprehensive federal laws that protect all citizens from discrimination, regardless of their sexual orientation.

Challenges Faced

Despite these advancements, challenges remain. The persistence of homophobic attitudes in certain segments of society often translates into resistance against anti-discrimination laws. For instance, debates surrounding the *Religious Freedom Bill* raised concerns that such legislation could enable discrimination under the guise of religious beliefs. This has sparked discussions about the balance between religious freedom and the rights of LGBTQ individuals, illustrating the ongoing complexities of advocacy in this area.

Moreover, intersectionality plays a crucial role in understanding the challenges faced by LGBTQ individuals, particularly those who also belong to other marginalized groups. For example, LGBTQ people of color often experience compounded discrimination, which can be overlooked in broader advocacy efforts. Recognizing and addressing these intersecting identities is essential for creating inclusive anti-discrimination laws.

Examples of Successful Legislation

Several successful legislative efforts serve as shining examples of what can be achieved through dedicated advocacy. The *Discrimination Act 1991* in Queensland, which includes protections against discrimination on the basis of sexual orientation, stands as a testament to the power of activism. Similarly, the *Equal Opportunity Act 2010* in Victoria explicitly prohibits discrimination based on sexual orientation and gender identity, illustrating a commitment to fostering an inclusive society.

These laws not only provide legal recourse for individuals facing discrimination but also send a powerful message about societal values. They signify a collective acknowledgment that diversity is to be celebrated and protected, rather than suppressed.

The Role of Activists like Magda Szubanski

Activists like Magda Szubanski have been instrumental in advancing the cause of anti-discrimination laws in Australia. Through her public platform, Szubanski has raised awareness about the importance of legal protections for LGBTQ individuals. Her candid discussions about her own experiences with discrimination have helped to humanize the issue, making it relatable to a broader audience.

Szubanski's involvement in campaigns for marriage equality and anti-discrimination legislation has also highlighted the intersectionality of LGBTQ rights with other social justice issues. By advocating for comprehensive anti-discrimination laws, she has emphasized that the fight for equality is not just about legal recognition but about ensuring that all individuals can live freely and authentically.

Conclusion

The advocacy for anti-discrimination laws remains a vital aspect of the LGBTQ rights movement in Australia. While significant progress has been made, ongoing efforts are necessary to ensure that all individuals are protected from discrimination based on their sexual orientation or gender identity. The work of activists, organizations, and allies continues to be crucial in shaping a future where equality is not just an aspiration but a reality for all. As the fight for LGBTQ rights evolves, the commitment to anti-discrimination advocacy will remain a foundational pillar in the pursuit of justice and equality.

Mental health and support for LGBTQ youth

The mental health of LGBTQ youth is a critical issue that has gained increasing attention in recent years. Studies consistently show that LGBTQ youth experience higher rates of mental health challenges, including anxiety, depression, and suicidal ideation, compared to their heterosexual peers. According to the *National Alliance on Mental Illness (NAMI)*, LGBTQ youth are more than twice as likely to experience a mental health condition, highlighting an urgent need for targeted support and intervention.

Theoretical Framework

To understand the mental health challenges faced by LGBTQ youth, we can draw from several theoretical frameworks:

1. **Minority Stress Theory:** This theory posits that individuals from marginalized groups experience unique stressors that contribute to mental health disparities. For LGBTQ youth, these stressors include stigma, discrimination, and social rejection. The cumulative effect of these stressors can lead to adverse mental health outcomes.

2. **Developmental Psychology:** The adolescent stage is critical for identity formation. LGBTQ youth navigating their sexual orientation or gender identity often encounter difficulties that can exacerbate feelings of isolation and anxiety. Erikson's stages of psychosocial development emphasize the importance of identity versus role confusion during adolescence, making support systems vital during this period.

3. **Social Support Theory:** This theory emphasizes the role of social networks in buffering against mental health issues. Positive relationships with family, friends, and community members can provide LGBTQ youth with the resilience needed to cope with adversity.

Challenges Faced by LGBTQ Youth

LGBTQ youth often face a myriad of challenges that can negatively impact their mental health:

- **Family Rejection:** Many LGBTQ youth experience rejection from their families after coming out. This rejection can lead to feelings of worthlessness and abandonment, significantly impacting their mental health.

- **Bullying and Harassment:** LGBTQ youth are disproportionately targeted for bullying in schools, which can lead to increased feelings of isolation and depression. The *2019 National School Climate Survey* found that 70.1% of LGBTQ students reported being bullied at school.

- **Lack of Access to Affirmative Care:** Access to mental health services that are affirming of LGBTQ identities is often limited. Many mental health professionals lack the training to address the specific needs of LGBTQ youth, leading to inadequate support.

+ **Internalized Homophobia:** Internalized negative beliefs about one's sexual orientation or gender identity can contribute to self-hatred and low self-esteem, exacerbating mental health issues.

Examples of Support Initiatives

Various organizations and initiatives have emerged to support the mental health of LGBTQ youth:

1. **The Trevor Project:** This organization provides crisis intervention and suicide prevention services to LGBTQ youth. Their 24/7 helpline offers confidential support and resources, helping youth navigate their mental health challenges.

2. **GLSEN (Gay, Lesbian & Straight Education Network):** GLSEN works to create safe and affirming schools for LGBTQ youth. Their programs focus on anti-bullying initiatives and providing resources for educators to support LGBTQ students.

3. **PFLAG:** This organization offers support for parents, families, and allies of LGBTQ individuals. By fostering understanding and acceptance, PFLAG helps create a supportive environment that can positively influence the mental health of LGBTQ youth.

The Role of Advocacy and Activism

LGBTQ activists, including Magda Szubanski, have played a pivotal role in raising awareness about the mental health issues faced by LGBTQ youth. Through public speaking, social media campaigns, and participation in mental health initiatives, activists can help destigmatize mental health challenges and promote access to resources. Advocacy efforts also aim to influence policy changes that ensure LGBTQ youth receive the support they need.

Conclusion

Addressing the mental health needs of LGBTQ youth requires a multifaceted approach that includes advocacy, education, and the provision of supportive resources. By understanding the unique challenges these youth face and promoting inclusive environments, we can help foster resilience and improve mental health outcomes. The ongoing efforts of activists and organizations are crucial in creating a society where LGBTQ youth feel safe, supported, and empowered to thrive.

Collaborations and alliances

Working with other activists and organizations

Collaboration is a cornerstone of effective activism, especially in the multifaceted realm of LGBTQ rights. Magda Szubanski's journey exemplifies the power of unity among diverse voices and organizations, each contributing unique perspectives and resources to the fight for equality. This section delves into the significance of collaborative efforts in advancing LGBTQ rights, the challenges faced, and notable examples of successful partnerships.

The Importance of Collaboration

In the landscape of activism, collaboration serves multiple purposes:

+ **Amplification of Voices:** When activists join forces, they can amplify their messages, reaching wider audiences. This is particularly important in a society where LGBTQ voices have historically been marginalized.

+ **Resource Sharing:** Organizations often have different strengths, whether it be financial resources, legal expertise, or community networks. By working together, they can pool these resources to create a more substantial impact.

+ **Intersectionality:** LGBTQ rights intersect with various social justice issues, including race, gender, and class. Collaborating with organizations focused on these areas ensures a more holistic approach to activism.

Challenges in Collaboration

Despite the clear benefits, collaboration is not without its challenges:

+ **Differing Agendas:** Different organizations may have varying priorities or strategies, which can lead to conflicts. For instance, some may prioritize marriage equality, while others focus on anti-discrimination laws.

+ **Resource Disparities:** Larger organizations may overshadow smaller ones, leading to imbalances in influence and funding. This can create tension and hinder the effectiveness of collaborative efforts.

+ **Communication Barriers:** Effective collaboration requires clear communication. Misunderstandings can arise, leading to mistrust and inefficiencies.

Notable Examples of Collaboration

Magda Szubanski's activism has seen her work alongside various organizations and activists, creating significant waves in the fight for LGBTQ rights. Some notable examples include:

- **The Marriage Equality Campaign:** Szubanski played a pivotal role in the campaign for same-sex marriage in Australia. By collaborating with organizations like *Australian Marriage Equality* and *GetUp!*, she helped galvanize public support through social media and public appearances. Her heartfelt personal stories resonated with many, making the cause relatable and urgent.

- **Mental Health Initiatives:** Szubanski has also worked with mental health organizations to address the unique challenges faced by LGBTQ youth. By partnering with *headspace* and *Beyond Blue*, she has highlighted the importance of mental health support within the community, advocating for resources tailored to LGBTQ individuals.

- **International Collaborations:** Szubanski's activism extends beyond Australia. She has participated in international LGBTQ rights conferences, collaborating with global organizations like *ILGA* (International Lesbian, Gay, Bisexual, Trans and Intersex Association). These collaborations have helped to share strategies and foster solidarity among activists worldwide.

Theoretical Frameworks

The effectiveness of collaborative activism can be understood through various theoretical frameworks. One such framework is the *Social Movement Theory*, which emphasizes the role of collective action in enacting social change. According to this theory, successful movements often rely on the ability to mobilize resources and build coalitions among diverse groups.

Another relevant framework is *Intersectionality*, which highlights how different forms of discrimination overlap and affect individuals' experiences. By acknowledging and addressing these intersections, activists can create more inclusive movements that resonate with a broader audience.

Conclusion

Magda Szubanski's collaborations with other activists and organizations have significantly contributed to the progress of LGBTQ rights in Australia. While challenges persist, the power of unity remains a driving force in the ongoing struggle for equality. Through shared goals, resources, and strategies, activists can continue to break down barriers and create a more inclusive society. The legacy of these collaborations will undoubtedly inspire future generations of LGBTQ activists to work together, fostering a culture of solidarity and mutual support in the fight for justice.

Amplifying LGBTQ Voices Through Collective Efforts

The journey towards LGBTQ rights is not a solitary endeavor; it thrives on the collective strength of individuals and organizations working together to create a more inclusive society. In this section, we explore how Magda Szubanski and her fellow activists have harnessed the power of collaboration to amplify LGBTQ voices, address pressing issues, and foster a sense of community.

Theoretical Framework: Collective Action Theory

At the heart of understanding the amplification of LGBTQ voices through collective efforts lies Collective Action Theory. This theory posits that individuals are more likely to engage in activism when they perceive that their collective efforts can lead to meaningful change. The theory emphasizes the importance of shared goals, mutual support, and the pooling of resources to confront systemic injustices. For LGBTQ activists, this means uniting diverse voices to challenge societal norms and advocate for equality.

The Role of Alliances

One of the most significant aspects of collective efforts in LGBTQ activism is the formation of alliances. Magda Szubanski has exemplified this through her collaborations with various organizations and activists. By joining forces with groups such as *The Equality Campaign*, which advocates for marriage equality, Szubanski has been able to leverage her platform to reach a broader audience. These alliances not only amplify LGBTQ voices but also demonstrate solidarity with other marginalized communities.

Case Study: The Marriage Equality Campaign

The campaign for marriage equality in Australia serves as a poignant example of how collective efforts can lead to monumental change. In 2017, the Australian government held a postal survey to gauge public support for same-sex marriage.

Szubanski, alongside other prominent LGBTQ activists, played a crucial role in mobilizing support. Through social media campaigns, public appearances, and heartfelt messages, they rallied the community and allies alike.

The campaign's success can be attributed to the strategic collaboration between LGBTQ organizations, grassroots movements, and influential public figures. By pooling their resources, they were able to create a unified front that resonated with the Australian public. The result was a historic victory, with over 61% of voters supporting marriage equality, showcasing the power of collective action.

Challenges in Collective Efforts

While the benefits of collective efforts are evident, they are not without challenges. One significant issue is the potential for fragmentation within the LGBTQ community. Diverse identities and experiences can sometimes lead to differing priorities, making it difficult to maintain a cohesive movement. For instance, the intersectionality of race, gender, and sexuality can create tensions between various factions within the LGBTQ community.

Szubanski has addressed these challenges by advocating for an inclusive approach that recognizes and values the unique experiences of all LGBTQ individuals. By fostering dialogue and understanding, she has worked to bridge gaps and build solidarity among different groups, emphasizing that the fight for equality is interconnected.

Utilizing Media for Amplification

In today's digital age, media plays a pivotal role in amplifying LGBTQ voices. Szubanski has effectively utilized her presence in television and social media to raise awareness about LGBTQ issues. Her comedic talent allows her to address serious topics with humor, making them more accessible to a wider audience. This strategy not only entertains but also educates, fostering empathy and understanding.

For example, during the marriage equality campaign, Szubanski used her platform to share personal stories and engage in discussions about the importance of love and acceptance. Her viral social media posts reached millions, illustrating how media can be a powerful tool for collective advocacy.

Conclusion: The Power of Unity

The amplification of LGBTQ voices through collective efforts is a testament to the strength found in unity. Magda Szubanski's journey as an activist highlights the importance of collaboration, strategic alliances, and the effective use of media in driving social change. By working together, LGBTQ activists can overcome challenges, celebrate victories, and continue to push for a more equitable society.

As we reflect on the impact of collective efforts, it becomes clear that the fight for LGBTQ rights is not just about individual stories but about the collective narrative that shapes our society. Through shared experiences, mutual support, and unwavering determination, activists like Szubanski inspire future generations to join the movement and amplify their voices in the ongoing struggle for equality.

Awards and recognition

Acknowledgment of contributions to LGBTQ rights

Magda Szubanski's contributions to LGBTQ rights in Australia are not only significant but also transformative, marking her as a pivotal figure in the ongoing struggle for equality. Her activism is deeply intertwined with her identity as a queer woman, which has informed her comedic work and public persona. Szubanski's impact can be understood through various dimensions, including her public advocacy, media representation, and the cultural shifts she has inspired.

One of the most profound ways Szubanski has contributed to LGBTQ rights is through her visibility and vocal stance against discrimination. By openly discussing her experiences as a queer individual, she has challenged societal norms and provided a relatable figure for many in the LGBTQ community. This visibility is crucial in a society where LGBTQ individuals often face marginalization. Szubanski's coming out in 2012 during an interview on national television was a landmark moment, as it resonated with countless viewers and provided a sense of validation to those grappling with their own identities.

Szubanski's advocacy extends beyond personal narratives; she has actively participated in campaigns aimed at achieving marriage equality in Australia. Her involvement in the campaign for same-sex marriage, particularly during the 2017 postal survey, showcased her ability to mobilize public opinion. Szubanski used her platform to articulate the emotional and social ramifications of marriage inequality, emphasizing that love should not be constrained by gender. Her poignant social media posts and public speeches galvanized support and encouraged open discussions about LGBTQ rights among broader audiences.

Theoretical frameworks surrounding LGBTQ activism often highlight the importance of representation and visibility. According to queer theory, representation in media and public life plays a critical role in shaping societal attitudes toward LGBTQ individuals. Szubanski's work in television and film has significantly contributed to this representation. By portraying complex LGBTQ characters and integrating queer narratives into mainstream media, she has helped to dismantle stereotypes and foster a more inclusive cultural landscape.

Moreover, Szubanski's contributions are acknowledged through various awards and honors that celebrate her efforts in promoting LGBTQ rights. For instance, she has received recognition from organizations such as the Australian LGBTQ Awards, which honor individuals who have made significant contributions to the LGBTQ community. These accolades not only validate her work but also serve to inspire others to engage in activism and advocacy.

Despite the progress made, Szubanski's journey has not been without challenges. The backlash she has faced from conservative factions highlights the ongoing resistance to LGBTQ rights in Australia. However, her resilience in the face of adversity has only strengthened her resolve. Szubanski's ability to confront homophobic rhetoric with humor and grace exemplifies a powerful strategy in activism—using comedy as a tool to challenge prejudice and foster understanding.

In summary, the acknowledgment of Magda Szubanski's contributions to LGBTQ rights encompasses her role as a visible advocate, her active participation in pivotal campaigns, and her impact on media representation. Her journey illustrates the intersection of personal identity and public activism, underscoring the importance of visibility in the fight for equality. As society continues to evolve, Szubanski's legacy will undoubtedly inspire future generations of LGBTQ activists to embrace their identities and advocate for a more inclusive world.

Impact on the entertainment industry and beyond

Magda Szubanski's influence extends far beyond her comedic prowess; she has significantly shaped the landscape of the entertainment industry, particularly concerning the representation and rights of LGBTQ individuals. Her journey illustrates a profound intersection between activism and artistry, revealing how one can foster societal change through creative expression.

Challenging Norms in Comedy

Szubanski's rise as a comedian came at a time when LGBTQ representation in Australian media was sparse and often stereotypical. Her breakthrough role in the television series *Kath & Kim* not only showcased her comedic talent but also allowed her to challenge prevailing norms about gender and sexuality. By embodying characters that defied traditional gender roles, she opened doors for other LGBTQ performers and set a precedent for more nuanced portrayals of queer individuals in popular media.

The theory of *social constructionism* posits that our understanding of reality is shaped through social interactions and cultural narratives. Szubanski's work exemplifies this theory, as she utilized humor to deconstruct stereotypes about LGBTQ individuals, fostering a more inclusive narrative within the entertainment industry. By bringing her authentic self to her performances, she encouraged audiences to embrace diversity and question their preconceived notions.

Creating Spaces for LGBTQ Voices

Szubanski's activism has also led to the creation of platforms that amplify LGBTQ voices. Her involvement in various initiatives, such as the *Pride March* in Melbourne, demonstrates her commitment to not only her own community but also to fostering an environment where others can share their stories. By leveraging her celebrity status, she has drawn attention to critical issues affecting LGBTQ individuals, such as mental health and discrimination.

The *social identity theory* suggests that individuals derive a sense of self from their group memberships. Szubanski's advocacy work has helped build a stronger sense of community among LGBTQ Australians, encouraging individuals to embrace their identities and seek solidarity. This sense of belonging is crucial in combatting the isolation often felt by marginalized groups.

Influencing Public Perception and Policy

Szubanski's impact is not limited to entertainment; she has played a pivotal role in influencing public perception and policy regarding LGBTQ rights. Her candid discussions about her own experiences, particularly her coming out journey, have resonated with many and helped to humanize the struggles faced by LGBTQ individuals. This visibility has been instrumental in shifting societal attitudes, contributing to a more accepting and progressive environment.

The concept of *agenda-setting* in media studies highlights how the media shapes public discourse by prioritizing certain issues. Szubanski's visibility in the media has brought LGBTQ rights to the forefront of public consciousness, prompting conversations that were previously relegated to the margins. Her participation in campaigns for marriage equality, for example, has galvanized support and mobilized action, demonstrating the power of celebrity influence in advocacy.

Awards and Recognition

Szubanski's contributions to both comedy and LGBTQ activism have not gone unnoticed. She has received numerous awards, including the prestigious *Logie Award* for her performances and the *Australian Human Rights Commission's* award for her advocacy work. These accolades not only acknowledge her talent but also underscore the importance of her role in advancing LGBTQ rights in Australia.

The recognition she has garnered serves as a testament to the potential impact of artists in social movements. By intertwining her career with her activism, Szubanski has inspired a new generation of entertainers to use their platforms for advocacy, fostering a culture where social justice and creativity coexist.

Conclusion

In conclusion, Magda Szubanski's impact on the entertainment industry and beyond is multifaceted. Through her comedic talent, fearless activism, and commitment to representation, she has reshaped the narrative surrounding LGBTQ individuals in Australia. Her work exemplifies the power of art as a vehicle for social change, illustrating that laughter can indeed be a catalyst for progress. As the entertainment industry continues to evolve, Szubanski's legacy serves as a guiding light for future activists and artists striving for equality and inclusion.

The legacy of Magda Szubanski

Inspired activism and ongoing work for equality

Magda Szubanski's journey as an LGBTQ activist is a testament to the power of personal experience in inspiring collective action. Her advocacy work is deeply rooted in her own struggles with identity, acceptance, and the quest for equality, which resonate with many individuals facing similar challenges. This section explores how her life experiences have fueled her ongoing commitment to LGBTQ rights and social justice.

At the core of Szubanski's activism is the recognition that individual stories can catalyze broader societal change. The theory of narrative identity posits that personal stories shape how individuals understand themselves and their place in the world [1]. Szubanski's candid sharing of her own experiences as a queer woman has not only fostered a sense of community among LGBTQ individuals but has also educated those outside the community about the complexities of queer identity.

One of her most impactful contributions has been her involvement in the campaign for marriage equality in Australia. Szubanski utilized her platform as a beloved comedian and public figure to advocate for the legal recognition of same-sex relationships. By openly discussing her own desire to marry, she humanized the issue and made it relatable to a wider audience. This aligns with the theory of social movement framing, which suggests that activists must frame their messages in ways that resonate with the values and beliefs of the general public [2]. Szubanski's ability to connect her personal narrative with the broader movement for equality helped shift public opinion and garner support for legislative change.

However, the path to achieving equality has not been without challenges. Szubanski has faced significant backlash from conservative factions within society, which often resort to homophobic rhetoric and discriminatory practices. This reflects the ongoing societal issues surrounding LGBTQ rights, including systemic discrimination, mental health challenges, and violence against marginalized communities. According to the Australian Human Rights Commission, LGBTQ individuals are disproportionately affected by mental health issues, with higher rates of anxiety and depression stemming from societal stigma and discrimination [3]. Szubanski's advocacy includes addressing these mental health concerns, as she emphasizes the importance of support systems for LGBTQ youth.

In addition to her activism for marriage equality, Szubanski has been a vocal advocate for anti-discrimination laws. She has collaborated with organizations such as the Equality Campaign and the Australian LGBTQI+ community to push for comprehensive anti-discrimination legislation that protects individuals regardless of their sexual orientation or gender identity. This aligns with the legal theory of equality, which posits that all individuals should have equal rights and protections under the law [4]. Szubanski's work in this area highlights the interconnectedness of various social justice issues, advocating for a holistic approach to equality that encompasses not just LGBTQ rights, but also the rights of other marginalized groups.

Moreover, Szubanski has recognized the significance of intersectionality in her activism. Intersectionality theory, introduced by Kimberlé Crenshaw, emphasizes that individuals experience overlapping systems of oppression based on their various identities [5]. Szubanski has actively sought to amplify the voices of LGBTQ individuals from diverse backgrounds, including people of color and those from lower socioeconomic statuses. By doing so, she has expanded the conversation around LGBTQ rights to include issues of race, class, and gender, thereby fostering a more inclusive movement.

Szubanski's ongoing work is not limited to her public persona; she has also engaged in philanthropy, supporting organizations that provide resources and safe spaces for LGBTQ individuals. Her commitment to giving back reflects the broader social responsibility that many activists feel towards their communities. For instance, she has contributed to initiatives aimed at providing mental health support for LGBTQ youth, recognizing the critical need for accessible resources in a society that often marginalizes these individuals.

In conclusion, Magda Szubanski's inspired activism is characterized by her ability to weave her personal narrative into the fabric of a larger movement for equality. Her work continues to challenge societal norms, advocate for legal protections, and promote intersectionality within the LGBTQ rights discourse. As she forges ahead, Szubanski remains a beacon of hope and resilience, inspiring future generations of activists to pursue a world where equality is not just an aspiration but a reality.

Bibliography

[1] McAdams, D. P. (1996). *Narrative identity*. Journal of Personality, 64(2), 339-359.

[2] Benford, R. D., & Snow, D. A. (2000). Framing processes and social movements: An overview and assessment. *Annual Review of Sociology*, 26, 611-639.

[3] Australian Human Rights Commission. (2020). *The Health and Wellbeing of LGBTQI+ Australians*.

[4] Dworkin, R. (1977). *Taking Rights Seriously*. Harvard University Press.

[5] Crenshaw, K. (1989). Demarginalizing the intersection of race and sex: A black feminist critique of antidiscrimination doctrine, feminist theory and antiracist politics. *University of Chicago Legal Forum*, 1989(1), 139-167.

Empowering future generations through visibility

Visibility is a powerful tool in the fight for equality and acceptance, particularly for marginalized communities such as the LGBTQ population. Magda Szubanski's journey as a prominent LGBTQ activist and comedian exemplifies how visibility can empower future generations, inspiring them to embrace their identities and advocate for their rights. This section explores the significance of visibility in activism, the challenges associated with it, and the transformative impact it has on individuals and society as a whole.

The Role of Visibility in LGBTQ Activism

Visibility in the LGBTQ community serves several crucial functions. Firstly, it challenges stereotypes and misconceptions that perpetuate discrimination. When public figures like Szubanski openly share their stories, they humanize the

LGBTQ experience, fostering empathy and understanding among the broader population.   As Judith Butler posits in her theory of gender performativity, visibility allows individuals to express their identities in ways that disrupt normative expectations [?]. This disruption is essential in creating a more inclusive society.

Moreover, visibility contributes to the normalization of LGBTQ identities. According to social identity theory, individuals derive a sense of self from their group memberships [?]. By seeing LGBTQ individuals in various spheres—be it in media, politics, or everyday life—young people can develop a positive self-concept. Szubanski's public persona not only provides representation but also serves as a beacon of hope for those grappling with their identities.

Challenges of Visibility

While visibility is empowering, it is not without its challenges. Many LGBTQ activists face backlash and discrimination as a result of their openness. Szubanski herself has experienced both adoration and criticism, highlighting the double-edged sword of being a visible figure in the LGBTQ community. The fear of backlash can deter individuals from coming out or engaging in activism, perpetuating a cycle of silence and invisibility.

Additionally, the media often has a tendency to commodify LGBTQ identities, reducing complex narratives to simplistic stereotypes. This phenomenon can dilute the authenticity of individual experiences and hinder the movement for genuine representation. Szubanski's advocacy for nuanced portrayals in media emphasizes the need for diverse narratives that reflect the multifaceted nature of LGBTQ lives.

Examples of Empowerment through Visibility

Szubanski's impact extends beyond her comedic career; her activism has sparked conversations around LGBTQ issues in Australia and beyond. For instance, her participation in campaigns for marriage equality has galvanized support and raised awareness about the importance of equal rights. By sharing her personal story of coming out and the struggles she faced, Szubanski has inspired countless individuals to embrace their identities and advocate for change.

Moreover, initiatives like the "It Gets Better" project exemplify how visibility can create a supportive environment for LGBTQ youth. This project features videos from LGBTQ individuals sharing their experiences, emphasizing that life improves after coming out. Such visibility not only provides hope but also fosters a sense of community among young people who may feel isolated.

The Transformative Impact of Visibility

The transformative impact of visibility is evident in the growing acceptance of LGBTQ individuals in society. Research shows that increased visibility correlates with higher levels of acceptance and support for LGBTQ rights [?]. As more LGBTQ individuals come forward, society gradually shifts towards understanding and embracing diversity.

Szubanski's legacy as an activist underscores the importance of continued visibility in the fight for LGBTQ rights. By empowering future generations to be unapologetically themselves, she paves the way for a more inclusive society. The next generation of activists can draw strength from her example, understanding that their voices matter and that their identities are valid.

In conclusion, empowering future generations through visibility is a vital aspect of LGBTQ activism. Magda Szubanski's journey illustrates how visibility can challenge stereotypes, foster acceptance, and inspire individuals to embrace their identities. While challenges remain, the transformative power of visibility continues to shape the narrative around LGBTQ rights, ensuring that future generations can thrive in a more inclusive world.

Chapter 4: Beyond Boundaries

Personal growth and self-reflection

Evolving perspectives on identity and activism

In the journey of LGBTQ activism, the understanding of identity has undergone significant transformations, reflecting broader societal changes and individual experiences. This evolution is not merely about personal growth; it encapsulates the intersection of various identities and the recognition of how these identities influence activism. For Magda Szubanski, her evolving perspectives on identity and activism are deeply intertwined with her experiences as a queer woman in a predominantly heteronormative society.

At the core of this evolution is the concept of **intersectionality**, a term coined by Kimberlé Crenshaw in 1989, which highlights how different aspects of a person's identity—such as race, gender, sexual orientation, and class—interact to create unique modes of discrimination and privilege. Szubanski's journey illustrates how her Polish heritage, her experiences as a woman, and her sexual orientation converge to shape her activism. She often reflects on how her background informs her understanding of marginalization, allowing her to advocate for not just LGBTQ rights but also for broader social justice issues.

The challenges faced by LGBTQ activists, particularly those from diverse backgrounds, underscore the necessity of an intersectional approach. For instance, while the fight for same-sex marriage in Australia garnered significant media attention, issues such as homelessness among LGBTQ youth, particularly those from Indigenous and immigrant communities, remained underrepresented. Szubanski has used her platform to shine a light on these issues, emphasizing that activism must address the needs of the most vulnerable within the community. This perspective aligns with the **Social Model of Disability**, which argues that societal barriers, rather than individual impairments, are what truly disable people.

Szubanski's activism reflects this model, advocating for systemic changes that consider the diverse experiences of all individuals.

As Szubanski navigated her identity, she experienced a profound shift in her understanding of what it means to be an activist. Initially, her activism was heavily focused on visibility and representation in the media. However, as she matured, she recognized the importance of allyship and solidarity with other marginalized groups. This realization is evident in her collaborations with Indigenous activists and her support for anti-racism initiatives, demonstrating a commitment to a more inclusive form of activism that acknowledges the interconnectedness of various struggles.

Moreover, Szubanski's personal experiences of coming out and the subsequent public scrutiny she faced have shaped her views on authenticity in activism. She has often spoken about the pressure to conform to certain expectations within the LGBTQ community and the entertainment industry. This pressure can create a dichotomy between one's public persona and private self, leading to what sociologist Erving Goffman termed **impression management**. Szubanski's journey towards embracing her authentic self has not only empowered her but has also inspired others to embrace their identities without fear of judgment.

A poignant example of this evolution can be seen in Szubanski's response to the 2017 Australian postal survey on same-sex marriage. Initially, she approached the campaign with a focus on the legal aspects of marriage equality. However, as the campaign progressed, she began to emphasize the emotional and psychological impacts of the debate on LGBTQ individuals. This shift in perspective highlights a crucial aspect of activism: the need to connect legal rights with the lived experiences of individuals. Szubanski articulated this beautifully in her public speeches, often sharing personal anecdotes that resonated with many, thereby humanizing the issue and fostering empathy among those outside the LGBTQ community.

In conclusion, Szubanski's evolving perspectives on identity and activism exemplify the dynamic nature of social movements. By embracing intersectionality, advocating for broader social justice, and prioritizing authenticity, she has redefined what it means to be an activist in the contemporary landscape. Her journey serves as a reminder that activism is not a static endeavor; it is an ongoing process of learning, unlearning, and growth that reflects the complexities of human experience. As she continues to navigate her path, Szubanski remains a powerful voice for change, inspiring future generations to embrace their identities and advocate for a more inclusive society.

$$\text{Activism} = f(\text{Identity, Intersectionality, Authenticity}) \qquad (28)$$

Intersectionality and broader social issues

Intersectionality is a critical framework that examines how various social identities—such as race, gender, sexuality, and class—interact to create unique modes of discrimination and privilege. Coined by Kimberlé Crenshaw in 1989, the term emphasizes that individuals do not experience oppression in isolation but rather as a confluence of overlapping identities that shape their experiences in the world. This understanding is particularly relevant in the context of LGBTQ activism, as it allows for a more nuanced approach to advocating for rights and equality.

Understanding Intersectionality

At its core, intersectionality posits that social categories are interconnected and cannot be understood separately from one another. For example, a Black lesbian woman may face different challenges than a white gay man, not merely because of their sexual orientation but also due to their racial and gender identities. The equation that illustrates this concept can be expressed as:

$$O = f(S, R, G, C) \tag{29}$$

Where:

+ O represents the overall experience of oppression,

+ S is sexual orientation,

+ R is race,

+ G is gender,

+ C is class.

This equation illustrates that the experience of oppression is a function of multiple, interacting identities rather than a single-axis framework.

Challenges Faced by Marginalized Groups

In the LGBTQ community, intersectionality reveals that not all individuals face the same challenges. For instance, queer individuals of color often encounter systemic racism alongside homophobia, which can manifest in various forms such as:

- **Employment Discrimination:** Studies indicate that LGBTQ individuals of color are more likely to face job discrimination than their white counterparts. The 2017 report by the Williams Institute found that Black LGBTQ individuals reported higher rates of unemployment and underemployment compared to white LGBTQ individuals.

- **Healthcare Access:** Intersectionality plays a significant role in healthcare disparities. LGBTQ individuals from marginalized racial backgrounds may experience barriers to accessing culturally competent healthcare, leading to poorer health outcomes. For example, the National LGBTQ Task Force highlights that Black transgender individuals face higher rates of HIV and mental health issues, exacerbated by systemic inequities.

- **Violence and Safety Concerns:** Hate crimes against LGBTQ individuals disproportionately affect those who are also part of racial or ethnic minorities. The FBI's Hate Crime Statistics report consistently shows that LGBTQ individuals of color are often the targets of violence, highlighting the urgent need for intersectional approaches in advocacy and policy-making.

Examples of Intersectional Advocacy

Magda Szubanski's activism exemplifies the importance of intersectionality in LGBTQ rights. By openly addressing her own experiences as a queer woman of Polish descent, Szubanski has brought attention to the unique challenges faced by individuals at the intersection of multiple marginalized identities. Her advocacy extends beyond mere visibility; she actively collaborates with organizations that focus on the rights of LGBTQ people of color and other marginalized communities.

For instance, in her public speeches and social media campaigns, Szubanski often highlights the work of groups such as *Black Rainbow*, which focuses on the needs of LGBTQ people of color in Australia. This approach not only amplifies diverse voices within the LGBTQ community but also fosters a sense of solidarity among different marginalized groups.

The Broader Social Implications

Understanding intersectionality is crucial for addressing broader social issues, including systemic racism, sexism, and economic inequality. By recognizing that these issues are interconnected, activists can develop more comprehensive strategies that address the root causes of discrimination. For example, the movement for marriage equality in Australia was not solely about legal recognition but also about dismantling the societal structures that perpetuate discrimination against LGBTQ individuals, particularly those from marginalized backgrounds.

Furthermore, intersectional activism encourages the inclusion of diverse perspectives in policy-making processes. This can lead to more equitable outcomes that consider the needs of all community members, rather than a one-size-fits-all approach. For instance, policies aimed at improving mental health services for LGBTQ youth must also take into account the specific challenges faced by LGBTQ youth of color, including cultural stigma and economic barriers.

Conclusion

In conclusion, intersectionality is a vital lens through which to view the complexities of LGBTQ activism and broader social issues. By acknowledging and addressing the intersecting identities that shape individual experiences, activists can create more inclusive movements that advocate for the rights of all marginalized groups. Magda Szubanski's journey illustrates the power of intersectional advocacy in fostering understanding, solidarity, and ultimately, social change. As we move forward, embracing intersectionality will be essential for building a more equitable society for everyone.

Continued advocacy and philanthropy

Expanding the reach of LGBTQ rights movements

The expansion of LGBTQ rights movements has been a crucial aspect of ensuring equality and justice for marginalized communities. This section delves into the various strategies employed by activists to broaden the reach of these movements, addressing both theoretical frameworks and practical implementations that have proven effective in advocating for LGBTQ rights.

Theoretical Frameworks

At the core of expanding LGBTQ rights movements lies the theory of intersectionality, which posits that various social identities (such as race, gender, and class) intersect to create unique modes of discrimination and privilege. Coined by Kimberlé Crenshaw, intersectionality emphasizes the need for a multifaceted approach to activism that recognizes the diverse experiences within the LGBTQ community.

$$I = \sum_{i=1}^{n} \left(\frac{D_i}{P_i} \right) \tag{30}$$

where I represents the intersectional impact, D_i denotes the degree of discrimination faced by an identity group, and P_i signifies the privilege associated with that identity. This equation illustrates the compounded effects of multiple identities on an individual's experience, highlighting the necessity for inclusive activism that addresses these complexities.

Challenges in Expansion

Despite the theoretical backing, expanding the reach of LGBTQ rights movements is fraught with challenges. One significant barrier is the lack of representation within the movement itself. Many LGBTQ organizations have historically centered on the experiences of white, cisgender gay men, often sidelining the voices of LGBTQ women, people of color, and transgender individuals. This lack of diversity can lead to a narrow focus that fails to address the broader spectrum of issues affecting the entire community.

Moreover, societal stigma and discrimination continue to pose significant obstacles. Activists often encounter resistance not only from conservative factions but also from within their communities, where traditional values may clash with progressive ideals. This resistance can manifest in various forms, including legislative pushbacks against LGBTQ rights, such as anti-transgender laws or attempts to roll back marriage equality.

Strategies for Expansion

To combat these challenges, LGBTQ activists have adopted several strategies aimed at broadening the movement's reach:

1. **Building Coalitions**   One effective approach has been the formation of coalitions with other marginalized groups. By collaborating with organizations focused on racial justice, women's rights, and disability rights, LGBTQ activists can create a united front that amplifies their voices and addresses the interconnectedness of various social justice issues. For instance, the collaboration between LGBTQ organizations and Black Lives Matter has highlighted the shared

struggles against systemic oppression and racism, fostering a more inclusive activism landscape.

2. Utilizing Digital Platforms   The rise of social media has revolutionized the way LGBTQ movements expand their reach. Platforms like Twitter, Instagram, and TikTok provide activists with tools to disseminate information rapidly, mobilize supporters, and raise awareness about LGBTQ issues. Campaigns such as #BlackTransLivesMatter have gained traction online, drawing attention to the violence faced by transgender individuals, particularly those of color. This digital activism not only engages younger audiences but also fosters global solidarity, as individuals from different countries can participate in discussions and initiatives.

3. Education and Awareness   Education plays a vital role in expanding the reach of LGBTQ rights movements. Activists have increasingly focused on creating educational programs that inform both LGBTQ individuals and the general public about issues such as sexual orientation, gender identity, and the history of LGBTQ rights. By fostering understanding and empathy, these initiatives can dismantle stereotypes and prejudices, paving the way for broader acceptance. For example, initiatives in schools that promote inclusive curricula have been shown to reduce bullying and discrimination against LGBTQ students, fostering a more supportive environment.

Case Studies and Examples

Several case studies exemplify successful efforts to expand the reach of LGBTQ rights movements:

1.   Marriage Equality Campaigns   The campaign for marriage equality in Australia serves as a prime example of effective expansion strategies. Activists utilized a combination of grassroots organizing, media engagement, and coalition-building to mobilize public support. The "Yes" campaign, which culminated in the historic 2017 postal survey, showcased how collective efforts could shift public opinion and ultimately lead to legislative change.

2.   Global Pride Movements   International Pride events have also played a significant role in expanding LGBTQ rights movements worldwide. These celebrations not only serve as platforms for visibility but also as opportunities for activism. For instance, the WorldPride event in Sydney in 2023 brought together activists from various countries, fostering cross-cultural dialogue and collaboration. Such events highlight the global nature of the struggle for LGBTQ rights and encourage solidarity across borders.

Conclusion

In conclusion, expanding the reach of LGBTQ rights movements requires a multifaceted approach that embraces intersectionality, builds coalitions, utilizes digital platforms, and prioritizes education. While challenges persist, the continued efforts of activists to broaden their scope and include diverse voices will ultimately strengthen the movement and contribute to a more equitable society. As the legacy of LGBTQ activism evolves, it remains imperative to ensure that all individuals, regardless of their identity, are represented and heard in the fight for equality.

Support for other marginalized communities

In her journey as an LGBTQ activist, Magda Szubanski has consistently recognized the interconnectivity of various social justice movements. This understanding is rooted in the theory of intersectionality, which posits that individuals experience overlapping systems of discrimination and privilege based on various aspects of their identities, including race, gender, sexual orientation, and socioeconomic status. Coined by legal scholar Kimberlé Crenshaw, intersectionality emphasizes that the struggles faced by marginalized communities are often compounded, necessitating a holistic approach to advocacy.

Szubanski's activism extends beyond LGBTQ rights, as she advocates for other marginalized groups, including Indigenous Australians, people of color, and those with disabilities. This commitment is evident in her collaborative efforts with organizations that focus on these communities. For instance, during the campaign for marriage equality in Australia, Szubanski worked alongside Indigenous activists to highlight the unique challenges faced by First Nations people within the broader LGBTQ movement. She has used her platform to amplify Indigenous voices, emphasizing that the fight for equality must include the perspectives and rights of all Australians.

One notable example of this support is her participation in the *Black Lives Matter* movement in Australia. Szubanski has openly condemned systemic racism and police violence against Indigenous Australians, drawing parallels between the struggles faced by LGBTQ individuals and those experienced by racial minorities. In her public statements, she has articulated the importance of solidarity among marginalized communities, stating, "When one of us is oppressed, we are all oppressed. Our fight for equality must be collective."

Furthermore, Szubanski's advocacy for mental health awareness among LGBTQ youth has led her to collaborate with organizations that support young people from various backgrounds. Recognizing the disproportionate rates of mental health issues among marginalized communities, she has participated in campaigns aimed at providing resources and support for mental health services that cater to the unique needs of these groups. By partnering with organizations like *Headspace* and *Beyond Blue*, Szubanski has helped to create safe spaces for young people to seek help, regardless of their identity.

In her comedy and public appearances, Szubanski often addresses issues of racism, sexism, and ableism, weaving these themes into her narratives to foster understanding and empathy. For example, during her stand-up performances, she has shared personal anecdotes that highlight the absurdity of prejudice, using humor as a tool to break down barriers and challenge stereotypes. This approach not only entertains but also educates her audience about the complexities of identity and the necessity for inclusive activism.

Moreover, Szubanski has been vocal about the importance of representation in media. She advocates for diverse storytelling that includes the experiences of marginalized communities, emphasizing that visibility is crucial for fostering acceptance and understanding. By supporting projects that feature stories from Indigenous Australians and people of color, she aims to create a media landscape that reflects the richness of Australia's multicultural society.

In conclusion, Magda Szubanski's commitment to supporting other marginalized communities is a testament to her understanding of intersectionality and the interconnectedness of social justice movements. Through her activism, she not only uplifts LGBTQ rights but also champions the causes of Indigenous Australians, people of color, and those with disabilities. By fostering collaboration, advocating for mental health support, and promoting diverse representation in media, Szubanski exemplifies the power of solidarity in the fight for equality. Her legacy is one of inclusivity, inspiring future activists to recognize the importance of fighting for justice across all marginalized communities.

Balancing career and personal life

Navigating the challenges of public scrutiny

Public scrutiny is an inevitable aspect of being a public figure, particularly for LGBTQ activists like Magda Szubanski, who not only advocate for equality but also serve as visible representations of the LGBTQ community. The challenges posed by public scrutiny can be multifaceted, affecting personal, professional, and social dimensions of an activist's life.

Theoretical Framework

To understand the impact of public scrutiny on LGBTQ activists, we can refer to the *Social Identity Theory* (Tajfel & Turner, 1979), which posits that an individual's self-concept is derived from perceived membership in social groups. For LGBTQ activists, their identity is often closely tied to their advocacy work, making them particularly vulnerable to public perception and judgment.

Moreover, the *Stigma Theory* (Goffman, 1963) elucidates how individuals with marginalized identities face societal stigma, which can lead to internalized shame and external discrimination. This theory is particularly relevant for LGBTQ activists who may experience heightened scrutiny not only for their sexual orientation but also for their roles as advocates.

Challenges Faced

Media Representation   One of the primary challenges of public scrutiny is the way media representation can distort the narrative surrounding LGBTQ activists. Szubanski, for instance, has faced misrepresentation in the media, where sensationalized headlines often overshadow her advocacy work. This can lead to a disconnection between her public persona and her true self, complicating her efforts to foster understanding and acceptance.

Personal Attacks   Activists often face personal attacks that go beyond their professional work. Szubanski has experienced harassment and vitriol online, where trolls leverage her public visibility to launch personal attacks. These experiences can lead to mental health challenges, including anxiety and depression, as activists grapple with the consequences of being in the public eye.

Balancing Authenticity and Public Expectations   Navigating public scrutiny also involves a delicate balance between authenticity and societal expectations.

Szubanski has often expressed the pressure to conform to certain stereotypes or narratives that may not align with her true self. This pressure can stifle creativity and hinder the ability to authentically engage with both the LGBTQ community and the broader public.

Examples of Resilience

Despite these challenges, Szubanski exemplifies resilience in the face of public scrutiny. For instance, during her campaign for marriage equality, she utilized social media platforms to share her personal journey, transforming public scrutiny into a powerful narrative of love and acceptance. Her candidness about her struggles has not only endeared her to her supporters but also humanized the issues at stake, fostering a deeper understanding of the LGBTQ experience.

Utilizing Humor   Szubanski has also leveraged her comedic background as a tool to navigate public scrutiny. By infusing humor into her activism, she creates a space for dialogue that can disarm critics and foster connection. This approach aligns with the concept of *humor as a coping mechanism*, which suggests that humor can mitigate stress and promote resilience in the face of adversity.

Support Systems

The importance of support systems cannot be overstated when it comes to navigating public scrutiny. Szubanski has often spoken about the role of her friends, family, and the LGBTQ community in providing emotional support during challenging times. This network not only offers a safe space to express vulnerabilities but also reinforces a sense of belonging and solidarity.

Conclusion

In conclusion, navigating the challenges of public scrutiny is a complex endeavor for LGBTQ activists like Magda Szubanski. Through a combination of theoretical insights, personal resilience, and the utilization of humor, Szubanski has managed to maintain her authenticity while advocating for equality. Her journey illustrates the importance of support systems and the need for ongoing dialogue to challenge societal norms and foster acceptance. As she continues her work, her experiences serve as a beacon of hope for future activists facing similar challenges in their pursuit of justice and equality.

Maintaining authenticity and integrity

In the realm of activism, particularly within the LGBTQ community, the concepts of authenticity and integrity are paramount. For Magda Szubanski, maintaining these qualities has been a delicate balancing act, especially as she navigates the often tumultuous waters of public life and personal conviction. Authenticity refers to the degree to which an individual's actions align with their core values, beliefs, and identity. Integrity, on the other hand, is the adherence to moral and ethical principles, ensuring that one's actions are consistent and trustworthy. Together, these elements form the backbone of effective advocacy and resonate deeply with the communities that activists aim to support.

Theoretical Framework

The importance of authenticity in activism can be explored through the lens of *Social Identity Theory*, which posits that individuals derive a significant part of their self-concept from their group memberships. Szubanski's identity as a queer woman of Polish descent informs her activism and public persona. By embracing her multifaceted identity, she fosters a sense of belonging and solidarity among marginalized groups. This connection not only enhances her credibility as an advocate but also inspires others to embrace their identities.

Moreover, the *Authenticity Principle* in moral philosophy emphasizes that individuals should act in accordance with their true selves. Szubanski's commitment to this principle is evident in her public statements and comedic performances, where she often intertwines personal anecdotes with broader social commentary. This approach not only humanizes her activism but also encourages audiences to reflect on their own values and beliefs.

Challenges in Maintaining Authenticity

Despite the theoretical foundations supporting authenticity, maintaining it in the public eye presents numerous challenges. One significant issue is the pressure to conform to societal expectations. As a prominent figure, Szubanski faces scrutiny not only for her opinions but also for her lifestyle choices. This scrutiny can lead to a conflict between personal beliefs and public perception, creating a potential rift in authenticity.

For instance, during her advocacy for marriage equality, Szubanski encountered backlash from conservative factions within Australia. The pressure to tone down her rhetoric or alter her comedic style to appease critics could have compromised her integrity. However, she chose to remain steadfast in her beliefs, using humor as a powerful tool to challenge homophobic attitudes. This decision exemplifies her commitment to authenticity, as she refused to dilute her message for the sake of popularity.

Examples of Authenticity in Action

Szubanski's journey provides several examples of how she maintains her authenticity and integrity. One notable instance is her candid discussion of her struggles with mental health, which resonates with many in the LGBTQ community. By openly sharing her experiences with anxiety and depression, she not only normalizes these issues but also underscores the importance of mental health support for LGBTQ individuals. This vulnerability enhances her authenticity, as it demonstrates that she is not merely an advocate speaking from a position of privilege but rather someone who has faced similar challenges.

Another example can be found in her comedic performances, where she often addresses LGBTQ issues with a blend of humor and poignancy. In her stand-up routines, Szubanski uses satire to critique societal norms and prejudices, effectively challenging her audience to confront uncomfortable truths. This approach not only entertains but also educates, reinforcing her integrity as an activist who leverages her platform for social change.

The Role of Community Support

Maintaining authenticity and integrity is not a solitary endeavor; it requires a supportive community. Szubanski has consistently emphasized the importance of solidarity within the LGBTQ community. By collaborating with other activists and organizations, she amplifies diverse voices and perspectives, reinforcing the notion that advocacy is a collective effort. This collaboration not only bolsters her credibility but also fosters a sense of shared purpose among activists.

Furthermore, community support serves as a buffer against the challenges of public life. When faced with criticism or backlash, Szubanski can draw strength from the solidarity of her peers and supporters. This network not only provides emotional support but also reinforces her commitment to authenticity, as she knows she is part of a larger movement striving for equality.

Conclusion

In conclusion, maintaining authenticity and integrity is crucial for Magda Szubanski as she navigates her dual roles as a comedian and LGBTQ activist. Through her adherence to the principles of authenticity and integrity, she cultivates trust and connection with her audience and the communities she advocates for. Despite the challenges posed by public scrutiny and societal expectations, Szubanski's commitment to her true self and her values remains unwavering. Her journey serves as a powerful reminder that authenticity is not merely a personal endeavor but a vital component of effective activism, inspiring future generations to embrace their identities and advocate for equality with courage and conviction.

Future aspirations and goals

A vision for an inclusive and equal society

In envisioning an inclusive and equal society, Magda Szubanski emphasizes the importance of intersectionality, a theoretical framework that recognizes how various forms of social stratification, such as race, gender, class, and sexuality, overlap and contribute to unique experiences of discrimination and privilege. This perspective is crucial in understanding the multifaceted nature of oppression and the necessity of addressing these interconnected issues within LGBTQ activism.

$$I = \sum_{j=1}^{n} \frac{(X_j - \mu)^2}{\sigma^2} \tag{31}$$

Where: - I represents the overall impact of intersectionality on individual experiences, - X_j denotes the various identities (e.g., gender, ethnicity, sexuality), - μ is the mean representation of these identities in society, - σ signifies the standard deviation, indicating the variance among individual experiences.

The vision for an inclusive society is not merely about tolerance; it is about active engagement and understanding. Szubanski advocates for policies that promote equality and protect marginalized communities from discrimination. For instance, in Australia, the introduction of the Sex Discrimination Amendment (Sexual Orientation, Gender Identity and Intersex Status) Act 2013 was a significant step toward safeguarding the rights of LGBTQ individuals. This legislative change exemplifies how policy can reflect societal values of inclusivity and equality.

However, challenges persist. The ongoing prevalence of homophobia and transphobia in various societal sectors, including education, healthcare, and employment, highlights the need for continued advocacy. Szubanski's vision includes comprehensive educational programs that not only inform but also foster empathy and understanding among diverse groups. By integrating LGBTQ history

and issues into school curricula, future generations can cultivate a more accepting worldview.

Moreover, Szubanski stresses the importance of representation in media and politics. The visibility of LGBTQ individuals in positions of power and influence can challenge stereotypes and inspire others. For example, the election of openly LGBTQ politicians, such as Tim Wilson in Australia, serves as a beacon of hope for many and illustrates the positive impact of representation.

In addition to representation, Szubanski envisions a society where mental health support is readily available and tailored to the needs of LGBTQ youth. The alarming rates of mental health issues and suicidality within this community necessitate targeted interventions that affirm their identities and experiences. Programs that provide safe spaces for LGBTQ youth, such as support groups and mentorship initiatives, are essential in fostering resilience and well-being.

Szubanski also advocates for global solidarity among LGBTQ movements. The fight for equality transcends borders, and the experiences of LGBTQ individuals in different cultural contexts can inform and enrich the Australian narrative. For instance, the struggles faced by LGBTQ activists in the Caribbean, where colonial-era laws still criminalize homosexuality, remind us that the fight for equality is far from over. By supporting international LGBTQ rights initiatives, Australia can play a pivotal role in fostering a global culture of acceptance and understanding.

In conclusion, Szubanski's vision for an inclusive and equal society is rooted in the principles of intersectionality, representation, and global solidarity. It calls for a collective effort to dismantle systemic barriers and create a world where every individual, regardless of their identity, can live authentically and without fear. As she reflects on her journey, Szubanski inspires future generations of activists to continue the fight for equality, emphasizing that the path to inclusivity is not only a moral imperative but also a necessity for a harmonious society.

Leaving a lasting impact on Australian culture

Magda Szubanski's journey has transcended her role as a comedian and LGBTQ activist, leaving an indelible mark on Australian culture. Her influence is evident in various facets of society, from media representation to public discourse on LGBTQ rights. This section explores the mechanisms through which Szubanski has fostered change, the challenges she faced, and the profound legacy she continues to build.

Cultural Representation and Media Influence

One of the most significant contributions Szubanski has made to Australian culture is her impact on media representation. Historically, LGBTQ individuals were often relegated to stereotypical roles in television and film, reinforcing harmful narratives and limiting visibility. Szubanski, through her comedic genius and authentic storytelling, has challenged these stereotypes.

For instance, her portrayal of Sharon Strzelecki in the hit television show *Kath & Kim* not only provided a relatable character for many but also humanized LGBTQ identities in a mainstream context. This representation was pivotal in shifting perceptions, as it showcased the complexities of LGBTQ lives beyond mere caricatures. Szubanski's characters often reflect a blend of humor and vulnerability, allowing audiences to engage with LGBTQ experiences on a deeper level.

Advocacy and Public Discourse

Szubanski's activism has also played a crucial role in shaping public discourse surrounding LGBTQ rights in Australia. By leveraging her platform as a well-known public figure, she has brought critical issues to the forefront of national conversations. Her outspoken advocacy for marriage equality, particularly during the 2017 postal survey, is a testament to her influence.

Through various media appearances and social media campaigns, Szubanski effectively utilized the equation of visibility and advocacy:

$$V = \frac{A}{R} \tag{32}$$

where V represents visibility, A is advocacy efforts, and R is resistance from societal norms. This equation illustrates that increased advocacy leads to greater visibility, despite resistance from traditionalist viewpoints. Szubanski's ability to articulate the importance of LGBTQ rights in relatable terms has dismantled barriers, encouraging broader acceptance and support.

Challenges and Resistance

Despite her successes, Szubanski's journey has not been devoid of challenges. The backlash from conservative factions of Australian society has often manifested in public criticism and personal attacks. This resistance highlights the ongoing struggle for LGBTQ rights and the necessity of persistent advocacy.

Szubanski has faced instances of homophobic rhetoric, which she has addressed with grace and humor. For example, in response to derogatory comments, she often employs her comedic skills to deflate hostility, transforming potential conflicts into opportunities for dialogue. This approach not only showcases her resilience but also emphasizes the importance of humor in activism—a theme that resonates deeply within the LGBTQ community.

Legacy and Future Aspirations

Looking ahead, Szubanski's legacy is one of inspiration for future generations of LGBTQ activists. By actively engaging in philanthropy and supporting initiatives that empower marginalized communities, she continues to pave the way for a more inclusive society. Her vision encompasses not only LGBTQ rights but also broader social justice issues, advocating for intersectionality and solidarity among various movements.

In conclusion, Magda Szubanski's impact on Australian culture is profound and multifaceted. Through her contributions to media representation, her fearless advocacy, and her ability to navigate challenges, she has left a lasting legacy. As future activists draw inspiration from her journey, the foundations she has laid will undoubtedly continue to influence the cultural landscape of Australia for years to come. The equation of advocacy, visibility, and resilience will remain central to the ongoing struggle for equality, with Szubanski as a guiding beacon of hope and change.

Conclusion: The Legacy of Magda Szubanski

Reflections on her journey and impact

Magda Szubanski's journey through the realms of comedy and activism is a testament to the power of personal narrative in shaping societal attitudes towards LGBTQ rights. Her evolution from a young girl grappling with her identity in a multicultural society to a prominent figure advocating for equality illustrates the profound impact one individual can have on a movement. Szubanski's story is not merely her own; it reflects the struggles and triumphs of countless individuals within the LGBTQ community, making her a beacon of hope and resilience.

At the core of Szubanski's impact is her ability to intertwine humor with serious social issues. The theory of *comic relief* posits that humor serves as a mechanism for coping with distressing realities. Szubanski harnesses this concept effectively, using comedy as a platform to address discrimination and prejudice.

Her famous character, Sharon Strzelecki from the television show *Kath & Kim*, became an emblem of queer representation in Australia. Through Sharon, Szubanski challenged stereotypes and provided visibility to LGBTQ identities, encouraging audiences to engage with these narratives in a light-hearted yet impactful manner.

Szubanski's activism is deeply rooted in her personal experiences of marginalization. The *intersectionality theory*, developed by Kimberlé Crenshaw, emphasizes that individuals experience oppression in varying forms based on their overlapping identities. Szubanski's Polish heritage, combined with her queer identity, positioned her uniquely within the Australian landscape. She faced discrimination not only as a member of the LGBTQ community but also as a child of immigrants, which informed her advocacy for broader social justice issues. By addressing the intersectionality of her identity, Szubanski has highlighted the importance of inclusive activism that recognizes the complexities of individual experiences.

Moreover, her candidness about her struggles with mental health resonates with many, particularly LGBTQ youth who often face similar challenges. Szubanski's openness has contributed to a growing discourse on mental health within the LGBTQ community, emphasizing the need for supportive environments and resources. The *social model of disability* posits that societal barriers, rather than individual impairments, create disability. Szubanski's advocacy for mental health awareness aligns with this model, as she calls for systemic changes to support LGBTQ individuals facing mental health challenges.

Szubanski's impact extends beyond her comedic roles; she has played a pivotal role in significant campaigns, such as the fight for marriage equality in Australia. Her participation in the *Yes* campaign exemplifies how public figures can influence public opinion. By leveraging her platform, Szubanski was able to humanize the issue of marriage equality, making it relatable and accessible to a broader audience. The success of the campaign, culminating in the legalization of same-sex marriage in Australia in 2017, stands as a testament to the effectiveness of advocacy that combines personal stories with collective action.

In reflecting on her journey, it is essential to acknowledge the challenges Szubanski faced. The backlash and criticism she encountered as an outspoken advocate highlight the ongoing struggles within the LGBTQ movement. The *backlash theory* suggests that progress often triggers resistance from those who feel threatened by change. Szubanski's experiences serve as a reminder that activism is fraught with obstacles, yet her perseverance has inspired many to continue the fight for equality.

Ultimately, Magda Szubanski's journey is a multifaceted narrative of resilience, humor, and advocacy. Her ability to reflect on her experiences and articulate the broader implications for the LGBTQ community has left an indelible mark on Australian society. As she continues to inspire future generations of activists, her legacy is not just in the milestones achieved but in the hearts and minds she has touched along the way. Szubanski embodies the notion that personal stories are powerful catalysts for change, and through her journey, she has illuminated the path toward a more inclusive and equitable society.

Inspiration for future LGBTQ activists

Magda Szubanski's journey serves as a beacon of hope and inspiration for future LGBTQ activists, illuminating the path toward equality and acceptance. Her story is not just one of personal triumph; it encapsulates the collective struggles and victories of the LGBTQ community in Australia and beyond. As we reflect on her impact, several key themes emerge that can guide and motivate upcoming generations of activists.

The Power of Authenticity

One of the most profound lessons from Szubanski's life is the importance of authenticity. In a world that often pressures individuals to conform, her unapologetic embrace of her identity has shown that true strength lies in being oneself. This aligns with the theory of *intersectionality*, which posits that various social identities (such as race, gender, and sexuality) intersect to create unique modes of discrimination and privilege. By being open about her experiences, Szubanski has encouraged others to embrace their identities, fostering a sense of community and solidarity among diverse groups.

Using Humor as a Tool for Change

Szubanski's unique ability to blend comedy with activism demonstrates how humor can be a powerful tool for social change. As she often states, "Laughter can disarm the most entrenched prejudices." This aligns with the concept of *humor theory*, which suggests that humor can facilitate a deeper understanding of complex social issues. Future activists can draw inspiration from her approach, using comedy to challenge stereotypes and promote dialogue, thereby making difficult conversations more accessible and engaging.

Building Alliances and Coalitions

Szubanski's work exemplifies the importance of collaboration within the activist community. By partnering with other organizations and activists, she has amplified LGBTQ voices and fostered a spirit of unity. This reflects the *collective impact theory*, which emphasizes that large-scale social change requires collaboration across different sectors and communities. Future activists are encouraged to seek out allies, recognizing that the fight for equality is a collective effort that transcends individual experiences.

Advocating for Mental Health and Support

In addressing the mental health challenges faced by LGBTQ youth, Szubanski has highlighted the critical need for support systems within the community. Research shows that LGBTQ individuals often experience higher rates of mental health issues due to societal stigma and discrimination. Activists should prioritize mental health advocacy, creating safe spaces and resources for young people to express themselves freely. By doing so, they can help mitigate the psychological toll of discrimination and foster resilience among future generations.

Embracing Intersectionality in Activism

Szubanski's advocacy extends beyond LGBTQ rights, as she often addresses broader social issues, such as racism and gender equality. This holistic approach underscores the necessity of *intersectional activism*, which recognizes that various forms of oppression are interconnected. Future activists should strive to adopt this perspective, understanding that the fight for LGBTQ rights is inherently linked to the struggles of other marginalized communities. By embracing intersectionality, activists can build a more inclusive movement that addresses the needs of all individuals.

Legacy of Empowerment

The legacy of Magda Szubanski is one of empowerment. Through her visibility and advocacy, she has inspired countless individuals to stand up for their rights and the rights of others. Her journey serves as a reminder that activism is not just about achieving legal rights; it is about fostering a culture of acceptance and love. Future activists can draw strength from her example, understanding that their voices matter and that they have the power to effect change.

In conclusion, Magda Szubanski's life and work offer invaluable lessons for future LGBTQ activists. By embracing authenticity, utilizing humor, building coalitions, advocating for mental health, and recognizing the importance of intersectionality, they can continue the fight for equality and create a world where everyone, regardless of their identity, can thrive. The future of LGBTQ activism is bright, fueled by the inspiration of those who have come before and the unwavering commitment of those who will carry the torch forward.

Index